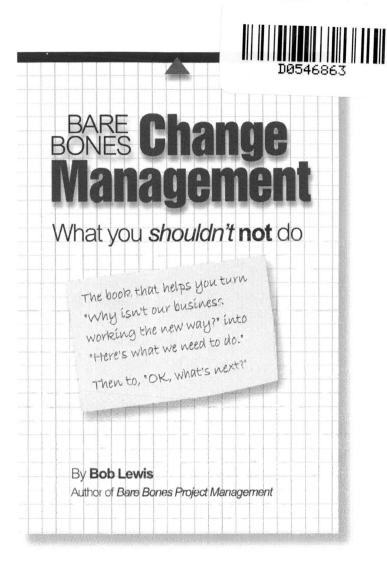

BARE BONES Change Management

What you *shouldn't* **not** do

The book that helps you turn "Why isn't our business working the new way?" into "Here's what we need to do." Then to, "OK, what's next?"

By **Bob Lewis**
Author of *Bare Bones Project Management*

♦S SURVIVOR
P U B L I S H I N G

6272 Sequoia Circle
Eden Prairie, Minnesota 55346,
(952) 949-2444

Visit our Web site at **www.issurvivor.com**

BARE BONES **CHANGE MANAGEMENT**

Copyright © 2010 by Bob Lewis
First printing: September 1, 2010

Published by **IS Survivor Publishing,**
6272 Sequoia Circle, Eden Prairie, Minnesota 55346,
(952) 949-2444.

Although the author and publisher have made every effort to ensure the accuracy and completeness of information contained in this
book, we assume no responsibility for errors, inaccuracies, omis-
sions or any inconsistency herein. Any slights of people, places or
organizations are unintentional.

ISBN 978-0-9749354-4-7
LCCN 2010935432

Design and production by Tim Bitney

DEDICATION

This one is for my father, Herschell Gordon Lewis. He was kind enough to make my childhood quite a lot stranger than what most of my friends enjoyed, courtesy of his being the "Godfather of Gore."

Being the son of, and occasional film crew member for the spatter movie's co-inventor gave me a certain cachet among my friends. I think it was cachet, although the worried looks my female classmates directed toward me suggest this wasn't as helpful in getting dates as I'd hoped it would be.

Much more than that, Dad is the world's acknowledged authority on writing persuasively (he calls it "force communication"). His guidance over the years has had a lot to do with whatever minor ability with the written word I've managed to bring to my trade.

CONTENTS

FOREWORD

I first met Bob Lewis many years ago, at one of those awkward alumni happenings designed by the school to collect your personal information for future fundraising efforts. It was a colossal bore for most of us; but of course, Bob was enjoying the event, meeting a few new people, but spending more time observing the activity than anything else. I introduced myself and discovered that he wasn't even an alumnus – just hanging around enjoying the food and people watching.

From that unique beginning, I've come to appreciate Bob's slant on the world. He always has a fresh, concise, practical approach to difficult business problems. Bob lives in the trenches, genuinely helping real people address real issues. His talent is an ability to take his ego out of every situation in order to find the right solution. Bob never feels the need to prove that he is the smartest person in the room – a challenge he would rarely lose – and is one of the most helpful people I know.

When I heard about this book, I was very excited. Twenty-eight years as a Change Catalyst puts me in great position to judge opinions on and approaches to change. My career covers companies from $3 million to $4 billion, in fields ranging from retail to operations, field and professional services, manufacturing, and consulting. Owners of these companies reaped more than $600 million of market value. It's a great perspective to judge a book on change and Bob is finally treading on my turf – a great opportunity.

Reader be warned! This is not an academic treatise! Bob's writing is always practical and insightful. If you wanted a comprehensive study on change, this isn't for you. Please return the book to Bob in the Twin Cities, or – better yet – pass it along to a friend because Bob really needs the exposure.

In any case, change is difficult. The only change most of us welcome is what we find in the sofa cushions or a vending machine. It's tough to break patterns and long-standing habits. Usually, the means for effecting change remain cloudy, even though the desired end results are clear. Rarely is there a sense of urgency to make change a reality. On top of all this, change can be dangerous to its advocates, often jeopardizing careers ... *or even lives!*

These conditions make it imperative to have great tools and insights in order to make the most of change situations. In that regard, Bob has done it again! His experience and ability to synthesize the best information from decades of experience has produced a great resource for veterans and novices alike. The book creates a practical and effective approach to change that untangles the key factors that make all the difference between success and failure. It supports that approach with numerous tools that ensure the critical steps are covered in any transformation effort. Bob takes a perfect scope – thorough enough to be complete, but not so comprehensive as to be smothering.

Bob takes a comprehensive overview of change. Normally, that would be an oxymoron, but in this case the book outlines process without entangling the reader in meaningless details. It covers all of the important factors to be addressed in any change effort without inundating the reader with trivial concerns. As a result, the book is a great how-to guide for novices facing their first change assignment; as well as a terrific reference book for the change expert.

Bare Bones Change Management holds a prominent place on my personal bookshelf as a reservoir of examples, processes, and worksheets that I can use in my change work. Often, just a few minutes' review of a chapter or two will stimulate new ideas and provide the frameworks that ensure that all the bases are covered.

Bob should have written this book 20 years ago! He would have saved me plenty of pain and aggravation. The book truly covers all the bases on making change happen in an organization.

From that knowledge, he put together a practical action guide and provided the worksheets and ideas necessary to succeed. It will be a crucial part of any change agent's library.

— Buckley Brinkman
President, Vallon LLC

PREFACE

This is a book about change, and how to be successful in achieving it. It's hardly the first book to be written on the subject.

What's the point of writing Yet Another Book for such well-explored territory? I have two. The first is contained in the title. As is often the case, once business change management became a consulting specialty it began to gain bulk. That's the nature of consulting specialties.

Without passing judgment on whether business change consulting specialists engage in overkill, I'm pretty sure most business change efforts don't need everything the specialty has to offer. In particular, I'm confident some of the pricier activities, such as "change readiness assessments" that survey employees and find, inevitably, that they are likely to resist change of all kinds, waste your time and budget.

After all, what are you going to do – read the results and say to yourself, "Well, if they're going to resist change, I guess we'd better cancel our plans"?

An earlier book, *Bare Bones Project Management: What you can't **not** do* (aka *BBPM*) left out most of what's known about project management, leaving only those elements without which projects have no chance of success. It's been popular and successful, and I mean that not only in terms of sales, but also in terms of what its buyers report: Projects run the Bare Bones way usually finish, more or less on time, more or less within their allotted budgets, and with the originally planned deliverables more or less intact. And, no minor point, without a death march at the end and with everyone still on speaking terms.

Even more important, they don't veer wildly out of control – if they do exceed their allotted time or budget, it's in a planned and orderly fashion.

But I was and continue to be concerned about a key omission. Projects are always about change, or what's the point? *BBPM* covers what's necessary for projects to *complete*, which is to say, get the deliverables out the door. *BBPM* talks about the difference between completion and *success* – achieving the planned business results – but doesn't provide guidance for how to achieve success.

The discipline of project management is, after all, about completion. Success is, for the most part, Someone Else's Problem, because the way these things are structured, business benefit begins the day after the project ends.

Put differently: Project deliverables are a means to an end – software, for example, that enables a business improvement. Projects complete when they provide their deliverables, which means the project team disbands just as their hard work is supposed to be put to productive use.

Putting it to productive use is the responsibility of whatever manager or managers are responsible for the business function that's supposed to become more effective. It is, in other words, an operational responsibility, not a project responsibility.

This book is a companion volume to *BBPM*. Unlike what *BBPM* covers, you certainly *can* not do what it describes. You probably *shouldn't* not do it, though (or, to the double-negative-challenged, you probably should do it). Business change management can make the difference between sterile completion and business success.

A second difference: Where BBPM left a lot out, this book is structured as a toolkit. It leaves less out, relying on you to use your judgment as to which tools you'll need for the business change you're managing.

A third difference: What made *BBPM* interesting was what it left out – everything known about project management except what you literally can't not do. I certainly didn't invent any of the techniques it described.

While I certainly won't claim everything in this book is original, it's as original as this sort of thing gets – it's a synthesis I've developed working with experts in the field, with my business partner, Steve Nazian, and with our clients over a span of more than a decade working with a wide variety of organizations on an almost-as-wide variety of business changes. If I'm not standing on the shoulders of giants, as Sir Isaac put it, I'm at least riding piggyback on a bunch of other toilers in the business change trenches.

That's the first reason for writing this book (or, from your perspective, for reading it). Here's the second, and more important one:

There are two schools of thought regarding resistance to change and what to do about it. The first, which overwhelmingly dominates the field, is that employees resist change because they're stupid, or, put more charitably, unenlightened. Because of this natural resistance, executives must push, drag, cajole, and otherwise expend mighty efforts so as to "unfreeze" the organization and institute change, before allowing it to "refreeze" into its new shape.

Based on my informal sampling of the literature, this just might be the first book ever written on the subject that's based on a different school of thought ... that employees resist change because they're smart.

The unenlightened employee model begins by telling us all change is good. Resistance to change is natural, we're told, hard-wired into the human nervous system as the result of millions of years of human evolution, but we all need to get past it.

But then, we're told a lot of dopey things. Sometimes resistance to change is, in fact, a good thing. It all depends on the nature of the change, and which side you're on. It's worth remembering that in World War II we called the good guys The Resistance. The agents of change? They were the evil ones.

About the hard-wiring: As it happens, my graduate studies were in the field of sociobiology – the evolution and neurobiology of behavior – so I'm confident I know more than our current cadre of business change management experts about what is and isn't hard-wired into the human brain. Yes, there is some hard wiring in the human brain. For example, the ability to learn language is a native capability. Bipedal walking is another piece of standard equipment, although the ability to simultaneously chew gum must be learned.

So there is some hard wiring. Not a lot, but some. Resistance to change? Not hard wired. Not even culturally ingrained. Everyday experience tells us the opposite is true. We no longer consider stone axes state of the art, for example, and beyond this, advertising copywriters would never slap the words "New and Improved!" on even the most minor of product enhancements if we all resisted change.

We like new and improved (even though logically it's impossible to be both). Anyone care to explain how something can be either new or improved without change happening somewhere in the mix?

Here's more proof – a simple experiment you can perform in the privacy of your own organization. Offer your employees an upgrade to a piece of core technology they use every day: Buy them a new car of their choosing. You'll pay for the gas, insurance, maintenance and repairs, and there are no strings attached.

Too over the top for you? Okay, smartphones for anyone who wants one; employees get to choose which make and model.

Or, company-paid premium-grade broadband to the home.

How many employees do you really think will resist any of these changes?

And yet, "everyone knows" all change is good and employees just naturally resist it.

That's the difference between scientific knowledge and business knowledge. Scientific knowledge depends on evidence, logic, and the rigorous testing of ideas in the laboratory and field. Business knowledge depends on the assertion of pet biases with great confidence.

Few people automatically resist change. If they did, CDs would have flopped, MP3 players would be oddities, Netflix a bit player, and Facebook an academic oddity. Heck, the entire World Wide Web would instead be the Nerds-Only Network.

For the most part, people don't resist change. What they resist is change they expect to be unpleasant, which is an entirely different matter. A lot of what's characterized as "natural resistance to change" is actually this natural resistance to the imposition of disagreeable circumstances, such as layoffs, longer work hours, the invalidation of hard-won skills, the redesign of responsibilities in ways that make work boring and dreary … in other words, the outcome of just about every business change employees have had to deal with over the past few decades. And here you come along with another one. In the absence of convincing information, what conclusion would you expect smart employees to reach?

Me too: That your change is going to be no better than any of the rest.

Your change is different, you say? Doesn't matter. What employees expect is what matters. And unless you provide convincing information, the change you're trying to institute falls into the class of events known collectively as "The Unknown."

Employees don't resist change, except for the unpleasant kind they mostly expect these days. They do, however, fear the unknown, and quite rightly, too. The nature vs. nurture question notwithstanding, it's easy to understand why the unknown is to be feared. Whether you imagine a Toe Monster lurking under your bed, a crazed mugger lurking in some dark alley, or layoffs lurking under the current process re-engineering effort in your company, the possible risks of the unknown – death, destruction and unemployment – outweigh most imagined benefits.

Before leaving the standard model behind, a word about its executive-as-change-promoter aspect: It's seriously flawed, in two respects.

The first: Frequently, employees who have terrific ideas for improving the business search in vain for an executive willing to invest in them. And second, executives who are interested in promoting important organizational changes usually find the greatest source of resistance to change isn't among staff-level employees.

It's among their fellow executives. That's because for employees, change might represent unpleasantness, but also might represent opportunity: They have more room to rise than they have to fall.

Executives facing change have to deal with the exact opposite – little personal opportunity; quite a lot of personal risk.

So this is the book you're about to read: A book about managing change that rests on these premises and inferences:

> People are, for the most part, rational, acting in their own self-interest.

> Employees resist change because they're smart, and because their experience with business change tells them the outcome most probably won't be in their best interests.

> The most significant resistance to change comes from within the executive ranks. This shouldn't be a surprise. For those near the top, the distance it's possible to fall vastly exceeds

the distance remaining to be climbed, so not every executive will see your change as a personal opportunity – some will see it as a threat. Couple that with the greater impact executive resistance can have and the accuracy of this proposition should be clear.

> The above being true, if you're planning a change and want it to succeed, you should follow an organized program of analysis and planning to define concrete actions that will minimize resistance ... and even more important, maximize support for ... the change you have to lead.

One more point is worth making. In his insightful book, *Managing Transitions: Making the Most of Change* (2003), William Bridges points out that no matter the nature of a change, even if it's widely understood to be beneficial to everyone concerned, employees are likely to resist or dislike the transition – the process through which the old goes away and the new takes its place. Transitions are where most of the hard work happens. They're also situations where employees inevitably experience a sense of loss, even when they expect the final result will be worthwhile.

Go back to the new car thought experiment: No matter how enticing the new car might be, some employees might still find the process of moving into the new car and going through the process of selling the old one to be aggravating.

And, some will have a sentimental attachment to the old car which will cause a feeling of regret.

Which is nothing more than a restatement: Employees resist what makes their lives difficult, not what makes their lives different.

Therein lies, not the problem, but the path forward.

ACKNOWLEDGMENTS

Where to start? Where to start...

I have to begin with my friend and mentor, Larry Robbins, who died tragically last year. Had Larry not made me aware that there is such a discipline as business change management, not only wouldn't this book exist, but very likely neither would my consulting business. *Requiescat en pace*, Larry.

Larry introduced me to the trade. David Kanally and Nancy Piro were my tutors at it when I was a consultant with Perot Systems, never once even hinting that it was an unsuitable discipline for an IT guy to add to his arsenal of techniques.

The methodology described in this book didn't originate in this book. It developed over time as a result of working with clients on a wide variety of changes. I'm constantly grateful to the companies that have chosen to work with IT Catalysts for their willingness to listen to our suggestions, their readiness to challenge and discuss, and their hospitality and friendship as we collaborate.

Nor have I been alone in this: My business partner, Steve Nazian, has helped me evolve, improve, sand, smooth and polish the techniques that follow ... and at times has been the one to remind me to practice them when I've become impatient to just get things done.

For the book itself, I'm indebted to Steve for his ability to "search and destroy" typographical errors as well as phrasing that's less than clear.

My wife, Sharon Link, deserves credit beyond her encouragement: As a successful business executive she has shared her experience in making change happen in quite a few companies, all of which are better off because of her efforts. This book is better off because of my willingness to take credit for the insights I've cadged from her when she thought we were just catching up over dinner.

Early in the writing of this book, your loyal author suffered a bit of insecurity as to whether it was worth writing. My friend Buckley Brinkman, who was kind enough to write the foreword for this book, offered the key words of encouragement: "If you don't think you have something new to say, don't write the book." That encouragement is the reason this book places so much emphasis on its most important premise – that employees don't resist change because they're stupid or unenlightened, but because they're smart.

Dave Kaiser, client, friend, and a talented CIO who makes business change happen as part of his job description offered too many excellent and practical ideas to incorporate into the manuscript to count. Beyond that, Dave was the one honest enough to tell me, after reading the first draft of Chapter 1, that it read like a textbook. If you find the book enjoyable to read, thank Dave.

Anita Cassidy, who holds the title of **Consultant Against Whom I Least Like to Compete** (and author of a number of excellent books on IT organizational effectiveness) shared a very large number of ideas and techniques. In a more just world I've have footnoted each one to give her proper credit. Instead, you'll have to guess.

Wayne Lindholm, president of the Scanlon Leadership Network, was kind enough to review the manuscript as it developed, providing both wise insights and enthusiastic encouragement along the way.

My old friend Stirling Rasmussen, former fellow-newspaper-man-turned-consultant from my Perot Systems days was also kind enough to review early drafts. Stirling's reality checks were very helpful in making this book ... well, more real.

As has been the case with every other book I've published through IS Survivor Publishing, Tim Bitney gets the credit for turning a bunch of words, figures and tables into something you can hold in your hand, read, and make sense of. More than that, he gets credit for not strangling your loyal author for including large tables that by rights shouldn't have fit between the covers at all.

And, for also making this our first book that's available in electronic form.

Finally, I need to thank everyone who reads ***Keep the Joint Running*** every week (www.issurvivor.com) and takes the time to either post comments or correspond. As a writer and consultant it's far too easy to end up one or two steps removed from the practicalities of day-to-day business leadership. To the extent the ideas in this book are useful and practical, their (your) willingness to share thoughts and experience are an important reason.

INTRODUCTION

Everything is easy until you do it. Then it isn't anymore.

Change shouldn't be so hard. The boss should be able to just say what he or she wants, and the business, like a well-oiled machine, makes it happen.

Some business leaders still think their job is to have the grand vision: "We're going to become a customer-focused company." If they're the hard-working sort, they might also spend time cheerleading the vision: They crisscross the country, visiting every store, branch office or remote location, giving a speech to employees that says, "We're going to become a customer-focused company."

Except that someone, has to turn "we're going to be a customer-focused company" into actionable changes in how the company designs, manufactures, delivers, prices, markets, sells, and supports its products – a far from trivial exercise. If those "leading" (in quotes for obvious reasons) the organization decide instead that everyone can independently figure out how the change will affect their different parts of the enterprise, the result will either be no change taking place, or vicious infighting as competing views of the change turn into incompatible realities.

Figure 1 tells the story: For change to happen – for a business to respond to a problem or opportunity – someone has to develop a solution, and create a plan to implement that solution. The solution and plan turn into one or more *projects* … the activities that turn the solution into organizational reality by following the plan.

Just pushing the organization is rarely good enough, though, because organizations by their very nature stabilize in a configuration that works.

You also need to pull. That's what business change management does … it helps pull the organization along the path to its new configuration.

Designing solutions isn't easy. It also isn't the subject of this book because that's what Lean, Six Sigma, Lean Six Sigma, Theory

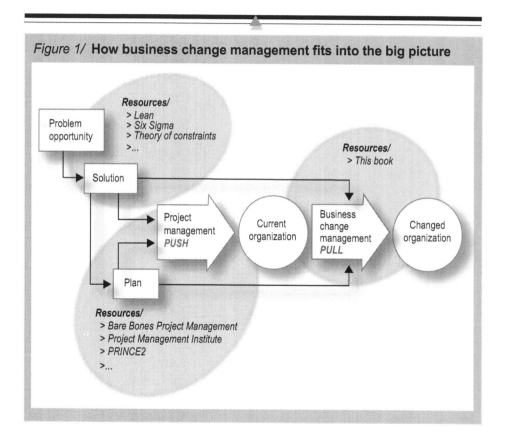

Figure 1/ **How business change management fits into the big picture**

of Constraints, Customer Relationship Management, the Rational Unified Process, and lots of other methodologies for figuring out better ways for the business to run are for.

If you aren't prepared for one of these formal disciplines, Chapter 3, on metrics, will provide some practical help, but that isn't why it's here. Its purpose is to help you stay focused on what to expect from the various solution design disciplines.

This book also isn't about planning change and executing the plan. If you want help with that subject, pick up a copy of *Bare Bones Project Management: What you* can't *not do* (hereafter referred to as *BBPM*). If you need more help than that, join the Project Management Institute and become a certified PMP, or adopt one of the rival project management methodologies and associations such as PRINCE2 or ASAPM.

Project management is the discipline you use to manage the tasks needed to complete a change. This book is a complement to that necessary discipline. You need it because even a small change – a new process to be followed by a single workgroup, for example, – can encounter resistance, and the challenge becomes progressively more difficult from there as the scope and size of a change increase.

That's where this book fits in. It starts where those other disciplines end: When the solution is ready to be turned into business reality and you're ready to start executing the plan.

CONTINUOUS IMPROVEMENT
THAT DOESN'T RUN OUT OF GAS

With sufficient insight and management skill, organizations can achieve the benefits of large-scale change programs in small increments. It's a highly desirable ability to develop.

If this is your goal, consider that the move from the type of organization you manage now to this "incremental transformation" style is a major change in and of itself.

This book will help you manage its implementation, just as it can help manage any other major change.

The magic buzz-phrase "Business Change Management" is the label applied to what you have to do so everyone (or at least, enough employees) accepts the solution and follows the plan. If you want a well-designed, well-planned change to become a successfully implemented change, it's a discipline you need to master.

Fortunately, doing so needn't be all that difficult. Mostly, it requires empathy; a structured method of attaching structure to your empathy, turning it into defined business change management tasks; and including those tasks in your project plan.

Here's one reason change is so hard: Most of the important changes businesses undertake mean choosing to experience some pain now so as to avoid more significant pain at some indeterminate time in the future.

Given a choice between pain now and pain later, human beings have a tendency to prefer later by a wide margin.

Here's how it works:

As Figure 2 shows, successful companies are more effective than their competitors in some respect that matters to the marketplace. Whatever this dimension of effectiveness, it is never sustainable in the face of stasis: The industry in which the company competes inevitably improves, reducing and eventually eliminating its advantage.

Companies can buy time … in some cases, quite a lot of time … by implementing what have come to be called "continuous improvement programs." Continuous improvement is a highly desirable ap-

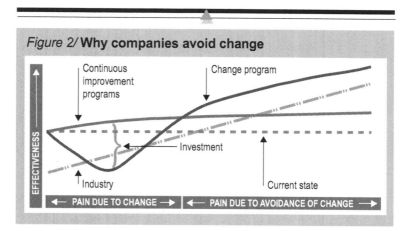

Figure 2/ **Why companies avoid change**

proach to change because it is relatively painless: It defines change in terms of small, easily achieved increments rather than big, difficult to digest gulps.

Think of continuous improvement as squeezing water out of a sponge. Squeeze the sponge, get water. Squeeze it harder, get more water. Simple. Straightforward. An easy way to cause the sponge to lose weight and become drier.

But eventually you reach the point of diminishing returns: You stop getting more water but do end up damaging the sponge. Similarly, continuous improvement programs eventually cease to yield significant improvements but can end up damaging departments pushed beyond their limits.

At some point, most companies, business units, departments, and workgroups find themselves at a point where a discontinuous *change program* is required to regain competitive advantage.

Change programs require two types of investment. The first is the tangible investment of time, money and staff that can be compared to projected benefits in a traditional return-on-investment (ROI) calculation. The second is less tangible but more important: During the change, the organization will lose effectiveness, because significant change:

> Takes staff time and management attention away from day-to-day operations.

> Creates worry and uncertainty among those who will be affected, distracting some from their responsibilities while causing others to seek and find employment elsewhere.

> Results in a temporary loss of employee effectiveness during the period in which they learn the new way of working.

One other point, which Figure 2 makes clear: The time to invest in discontinuous change is when the organization is still ahead of the competition and can afford a temporary reduction in effectiveness.

By the time the usual measures show a problem, it's too late. Companies in this situation have already been outdistanced by the competition. They've probably thinned out staff through layoffs in a vain attempt to "keep costs in line with declining revenue," reducing their capacity to institute the necessary changes. And cash is, by then, too tight to make the required investments.

Yet, executive compensation too seldom supports the long-range thinking required to invest in change before this loss of competitiveness becomes apparent. Quite the opposite – it usually rewards quarter-by-quarter improvements in profitability, however achieved. The usual outcome: When the first early warnings appear, cutting costs to "send a signal to Wall Street" is much easier than addressing the reasons the organization has begun to falter.

Put simply, when it comes to investing in significant change, most business leaders, at all levels, are rewarded for procrastination rather than anticipation.

We'll take up this subject in more detail in Chapter 4. For now, recognize it as a driving force behind organizational, as opposed to individual resistance to change.

CHANGE ROLES

When you're involved in a business change, it's worthwhile to understand the various actors who generally participate in making it happen. They are the business sponsor, one or more champions, one or more drivers, participants, and performers (also known as targets or, most honestly, victims).

As you'll be seeing these terms used throughout the book, here's a quick account of each:

Business sponsor

The business sponsor is the person who:

> Wants the change to succeed ... really wants it to succeed, deep in his or her bones.

> Has the authority to define success, which also means he or she has committed to the business benefit promised by the change.

> Has the authority to make different kinds of decisions and re-solve different kinds of issues ... and this includes budget au-thority, and the authority to approve changes to the schedule and scope of the effort ... and to delegate that authority when the situation calls for it.

The one inviolable rule of business change is, no sponsor, no *change*.

Champions

Champions are people who want the change to happen ... some-times even more than the sponsor ... but who lack the authority to make it happen on their own.

They do have the ability to influence, and are tremendously valu-able to anyone in your position...working to make change happen.

About champions: Very often, one of the champions is the em-ployee who first conceived of the change you're trying to put into place and sold the idea to the sponsor.

Occasionally, companies still make the mistake of recruiting a sponsor, which means the champion sold a high-level executive on the idea but that executive is either too busy or too important to per-sonally sponsor the change in question. So that executive recruits or appoints a sponsor, who doesn't really care all that much about the project.

Now you have a Sponsor In Name Only (SINO) – a very dan-gerous situation. If you're faced with this, work with both the SINO and the SINO's boss to turn the SINO into a real sponsor, or to find a replacement who's more interested in the effort.

Drivers

This is you – someone responsible for making the change happen.

You're a driver either because you're driving change into the organization (the forceful view) or because you're using the gas, brakes, and steering wheel to "drive" the effort to a successful conclusion.

Depending on the size of the effort, you might not be the only driver. If there is more than one, the change effort needs an administrative structure to coordinate all of your efforts. The specifics of how to build one are, however, beyond the scope of this book.

Pay attention, now, because this is very important: *This entire book is written for Drivers ... you.* If people in other change roles also find it helpful, that will be lovely. It was, however, written from your perspective, not theirs.

Participants

Participants are members of the project team or project teams who are working to make the change a success. This book isn't about them. *Bare Bones Project Management* was about them.

Performers

Performers, also known as *targets*, are the people who do the actual work in the business areas affected by a change. It isn't a stretch to call them *victims*, either – they're the ones who will have to pick up the pieces and figure out how to handle all of the myriad exceptions to the elegant process designs being put into production, replacing the workarounds they figured out to handle the exceptions to the old processes that are being replaced.

They don't have to be victims, though. That, in fact, is a big part of what Chapter 2 is about.

WHAT'S IN THIS BOOK

Seven major components to business change management. Seven habits of highly effective people. Coincidence? You be the judge.

In any event, the components of business change management, which also are the chapters of this book, are:

> *Stakeholder analysis:* Anticipating how different stakeholders will react to the proposed change, why they're likely to react that way, and what you plan to do in response to their reaction, whether favorable or unfavorable.

> *Involvement plan:* You're more likely to resist something I do to you than something we do together. The involvement plan takes advantage of this not-very-blinding insight.

> *Metrics plan:* The point of any business change is to alter the current reality into something better. The metrics plan is the answer to the question, "How do we know it worked?"

> *Structure plan:* The entire organization is designed to reinforce its pre-change way of operating. Unless you change the structural elements to support the new way of working, they will anchor you in the old one.

> *Training plan:* Employees know how to do their jobs the way the business is currently put together. They don't know how to do them the new way ... a major source of uncertainty, and, therefore, worry. A good training plan alleviates this uncertainty.

> *Culture change plan:* For many changes, a change in culture is a prerequisite for success. For most of the rest, a change in culture is a major component of the change. Two questions need to be answered: (1) How to go about characterizing culture, and (2) how to go about changing it.

> *Communications plan:* As already explained, a major source of resistance to change is uncertainty, which means employees have questions that need answers. They'll get their answers from someone. The only question is, from whom?

Those are the components of a bare bones business change management plan. The final chapter covers two other topics:

> *Integrating Business Change Management and Project Management:* Business change management consists of work, in the form of tasks that have to be coordinated with the rest of the work. That means you have to integrate business change management tasks into the project schedule.

> *Evaluation:* After the change is in place, the dust has settled, and the metrics plan has answered the question of whether it achieved the envisioned results, some important questions remain regarding how well the organization defined, planned, decided, and executed. The point of experience is to improve what works while making each mistake no more than once.

All this might seem like a lot. It is. And this is the bare bones version.

Business change management is a "non-trivial task."

CHAPTER 1/

STAKEHOLDER ANALYSIS

Most organizations have some sort of formal governance process to decide which business change proposals to approve. In some way, shape, or form, they are all driven by some sort of cost/benefit analysis (CBA) that determines the return on investment (ROI).
This makes sense: The only change efforts that get started should be good for the organization.

But change efforts don't succeed because they're good for the organization. They succeed when they're good for someone in the organization. ROI is the ante that gets you into the game. Personal benefit is what gives you a winning hand.

You're trying to accomplish something – to change the business in some way. Some people will like it. Some won't. The rest won't commit one way or the other (Figure 3).

The ones who will like it are potential allies. They can help you make it happen. Unless you alienate them, that is. If you do, they'll be the worst opponents you have because everyone else will understand that something changed their minds.

The ones who won't like it will work, with varying degrees of energy and cleverness, to make sure your change fails, or at least doesn't fully succeed. Leave them alone and their opposition will damage or ruin your efforts, along with your reputation for effective leadership. Co-opt them … convince them to support your effort … and their change of mind will be one of your most potent persuaders for everyone else.

Everyone else? Although they won't work to make you fail, they won't lift a finger to help you succeed, either. Mostly, they'll keep their heads down until the dust has settled and they know who it's safe to support. They're the organizational inertia you have to overcome to finish the job. They'll accept change; that's their limit.

But who are these people? You can't deal with generic change resisters, you might alienate supporters if you can't identify them, and you can't lead anonymous agnostics.

Which is why your first step in managing change is to perform a *Stakeholder Analysis* – an assessment of which individuals or groups are likely to support, resist, or keep their heads down during the change; why they're likely to respond this way; and what you plan to do about it.

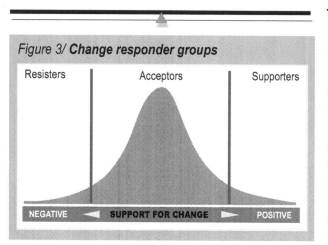

Figure 3/ Change responder groups

Resisters   Acceptors   Supporters

NEGATIVE   ◀   SUPPORT FOR CHANGE   ▶   POSITIVE

THE THREE RESPONDER GROUPS

In the absence of any action beyond the announcement of a change, executives, managers, and staff-level employees fall into three groups, separated by very fuzzy boundaries. These groups are your natural supporters, your natural resisters, and those who neither naturally support nor resist the change ... call them acceptors, because left to their own devices they'll accept the final outcome without exerting much energy to either help or hinder it.

A bit more about each of the three groups:

Natural supporters

Natural supporters are the folks who will make the difference between an organization that embraces your change and one you have to drag into it grudgingly ... and temporarily, because the ability of an organization to snap back to its original shape is remarkable.

"Natural supporter" refers to members of the organization who will support the change the moment it's announced. Their support doesn't come from any special action you've taken. They hear enough about the change to get a sense of what it's about and figure it will be to their advantage. So they support it.

Natural supporters will not experience much in the way of regret or loss as the result of your change, any more than they'd experience a sense of loss from a headache going away. They like what they think is going to happen and want to be part of it.

For a typical business change, figure between 10 and 20% of employees will start off supporting what you have in mind strongly enough to be of help.

The exact numbers are neither reliable nor important. They aren't reliable because they depend on the nature of the change and how strongly each individual feels about it. They also depend on where you draw the line that separates the three groups – the actual differences are as much matters of degree as of kind.

They aren't important because what matters is knowing that unless your change is particularly onerous, you'll find enough employees who support it to be helpful; not so many that you can ignore the need to plan for everyone else.

AS BASIC AS IT GETS: *Structure situations so that those who support your change benefit from their support, and those who actively work to subvert it experience ... negative reinforcement ... as a result.*

Where to find them

Look for natural supporters among ambitious executives and managers who have no stake in the old way of doing things.

Among staff-level stakeholders ("performers" in change-management lingo; although "targets" or "victims" are often more accurate terms) the most likely natural supporters are employees who have ambitions, complain about inefficiencies, and are confident of their ability to adapt.

To help you identify supporters, here are some phrases you'll hear from them but nobody else:

> We.
> What if we try ...
> Let's give it a try and see what happens.
> Let's figure out a way to handle this.

What to do with them

Whatever you do, don't think of your supporters – natural or otherwise – as followers to whom you can simply give assignments. That's a terrific way to alienate them. You need to nurture them. So involve them, give them leadership roles, compliment them, express your appreciation, and when circumstances allow it, give them promotions.

Natural resisters

While it isn't true that "employees" just naturally resist change, it is true that some employees do. More will resist the specific change you're trying to make because they expect it to be against their best interests. The reasons depend on the specific change you're trying to implement.

Whatever those reasons, these natural change resisters can, if ignored, subvert your efforts by encouraging others to resist the change as well.

In round numbers, figure you'll have as many natural resisters as natural supporters – between 10 and 20% in a typical organization and for a typical change.

These numbers are about as reliable as those provided for supporters, which is to say not at all. What matters is that except for particularly nasty changes (full functional offshore outsources come to mind), resisters will be an important minority, but not the main event.

For resisters, as the change becomes more and more real, they will experience a sense of loss … of how they're accustomed to working; of colleagues who will be laid off (or of their own jobs if they expect to be among the ones to go); of respect for hard-won skills; or of knowing the ropes.

And so, natural resisters go through the well-known five stages of grief: Denial, anger, anger, anger, and more anger.

Rational resisters

Many of those who resist your change will do so through more-or-less rational and logical analysis. They've reached a different conclusion than you because they began with different assumptions than you did, and perhaps interpret the evidence differently as well. Or, unlike you, they quite accurately expect they'll end up in the victim column when the change is done, either losing their jobs altogether or losing a lot of what they enjoy about their jobs now.

You can deal with resisters like this. You might even get them on your side, if you can persuade them the change is necessary and that they have a good chance of coming through it okay.

These change resisters will keep their emotions in check, unlike the other category of natural change resister, which is ...

Irrational resisters

This second group doesn't simply dislike a change as a result of rational analysis. Even if their resistance begins there, it ends up becoming an emotional response. They're angry. They need someone to blame. Worst of all, because they're angry, they back themselves into an emotional corner – changing their minds becomes increasingly difficult because it isn't in angry people to even consider other perspectives, let alone adopt them.

You'll have to take special steps for those who are stuck on anger – a subject we'll cover later in this chapter.

Where to find them

Look for natural resisters among the executives and managers who are likely to lose authority, control, influence, importance, or prestige as a result of the change. Even more, expect the ones who helped create the old way of doing things to be less than grateful that you'll be retiring the results of their hard work.

In highly political environments, resistance can result from old-fashioned favor-trading ... a factor that's particularly difficult to uncover and even harder to neutralize. Look for resistance from executives who have no obvious reason to object – this might be the reason.

In the performer community, employees who consider their old skills to be a key part of their value ... the skills that won't be important following the change ... are very likely to be unhappy about the change that makes those skills worthless (or worth less). To the extent employees expect the change to result in more work – especially if it's without better pay – you shouldn't be surprised when some of them decide they'd be better off if it fails.

An even bigger hurdle: Employees who are insecure about their ability to learn the new ropes will generally grip the old ropes pretty hard.

One more place to look: Employees who are Just Plain

Troublemakers. Not employees who agitate for improvement and complain about perceived problems … they're likely supporters. Just Plain Troublemakers are the employees who consider complaining to be a favored topic of conversation while having an infinite supply of reasons no solution will ever work. They are the chronic fault-finders, for whom the guilty party is always "them."

To help you identify resisters, here are some phrases to listen for. They're pretty good symptoms of change resistance:
> *They,* especially when used with no antecedent.
> "It's this year's management fad. Wonder how long this one will last."
> "It will never be approved."
> "Nobody asked *my* opinion about this."
> "It'll never work."
> "We tried this before and it didn't work."
> "This isn't new – it's what we've been doing all along."
> "We must have been doing something right all these years."
> "Back in the good ole days."

The phrases themselves are telltales. In particular, listen for them in the meetings that sometimes take place after the meeting … the hallway conversations that follow. Some of these will be debriefings among your supporters, analyzing what was said, what it meant, and how to respond.

Many more, though, will be the conversations in which resisters are honest among themselves after telling you what they figured you wanted to hear.

What to do with them

It's tempting to ignore change resisters, figuring they'll eventually shoot themselves in their feet, saving you the trouble.

It's tempting. It isn't, however, a winning strategy. Left to their own devices they'll poison the atmosphere, because acceptors are just as likely to take their lead from the malcontents as from you.

Here's what you can do with them: Ideally, you can co-opt at least a few, turning them into supporters (see *Give special treatment* and *Defuse* toward the end of the chapter). It's the ideal because no other advocate is as persuasive as a convert. Even better, their having publicly changed their minds makes it okay for everyone else to change their minds.

You won't co-opt many natural resisters, although you can turn many into acceptors … assuming, that is, that their resistance isn't based on an accurate assessment of what the change will do to them (as opposed to what it will do *for* them).

For the ones who are stuck on anger and aren't likely to get unstuck, isolate them, move them aside (what a friend calls a "lateral arabesque"), demote them, and if necessary, lay them off.

In a few cases, a public termination will be in order. It isn't all that common, but it does happen that an executive or middle manager will very publicly encourage employees to resist a change. Terminating that individual (who, his boss will announce, has "decided to pursue other interests") will send a useful message to everyone else.

(It's worth pointing out that arranging for the termination of an individual outside your own authority can be awkward, and always calls for political dexterity that might be mistaken for backstabbing. Be careful how you go about this sometimes-necessary step.)

One way or another, get resisters out of the way, not because they're bad people but because they're a bad fit for what the organization needs from now on.

Natural acceptors

Most staff-level employees, and managers and executives too, will neither naturally resist your change nor naturally support it. They'll wait to see if it all blows over and turns out to be the fad of the year.

They'll wait to see who the political winners and losers are, too. If your change isn't successful, you'll lose political clout while your opponents gain it, and they're smart enough to know that, if this happens, being too closely associated with you won't be a career-enhancing situation.

Anyone who isn't a clear resister or supporter is an acceptor. As you plan how to deal with acceptors, remember they will, with few exceptions, be dealing with a sense of loss … they'll be grieving even if they accept the need for the change to take place. The difference between acceptors and resisters isn't that one grieves while the other doesn't. It's that acceptors will go through all five stages of grief [1] and emerge on the other side.

---

1 Denial, anger, negotiation, depression, and acceptance. Although few will experience these in their extreme forms, most will experience them strongly enough to need your help maintaining perspective.

One of your most important jobs is to help them through the process – mostly by making sure they're aware that it's taking place (easy to do; hard to do without sounding patronizing).

The key to dealing with acceptors is that they need leadership, and will get it from someone. It could one of your supporters. It could be one of the resisters.

Or, it could be you.

PERFORMING THE STAKEHOLDER ANALYSIS

A stakeholder analysis divides the company into the individuals and constituencies that care, might care, or should care about the outcome of your planned change. In it, you do your best to anticipate whether each is most likely to be a supporter, resister, or acceptor; how much impact they're likely to have; the factors that put them into that category; and what you're going to do about those factors … to keep supporters on your side, recruit or neutralize resisters, and encourage or placate acceptors.

Let's walk through the thought process for a few stakeholders to get an idea of how to go about this. For each, the subjects are:

> *Who:* Identify the stakeholder (which might be an individual, or a group).
> *Status:* Whether you expect the stakeholder to be a natural supporter, acceptor, or resister.
> *Impact:* The extent to which the stakeholder's support or resistance will advance or hinder the change.
> *Support/Resistance Factors:* What it is about the stakeholder that lead to your assessment of his/her/their status.
> *Strategy:* What you plan to do to maintain the stakeholder's support/turn acceptance into support/deal with resistance.

How to define "Who"

Each "who" is either an individual stakeholder or a fairly homogeneous group of stakeholders.

Role-driven analysis

Most often, you'll develop your list based on organizational roles, roles in your change project, or both. Doing so is straightforward, except for situations in which a stakeholder group is likely to be divided in its response to the planned change. When that's the case, plan based on the response you expect to dominate. To the extent possible, deal with the exceptions as individuals, because you'll have a hard time formulating your other plans ... especially your communications plan ... to address different responders within a stakeholder group differently.

Examples of individual role-based stakeholders are the CEO, CFO, CIO, COO, and CMO (chief marketing officer, in case you haven't run across that designation).

Stakeholder groups might include financial analysts, programmers, marketing layout artists, and auditors, to list a few randomly chosen examples.

Subculture-driven analysis

An alternative to dividing stakeholders by role is to divide them by subculture.

We'll cover culture in more detail in Chapter 6. For now, think of business subcultures as archetypes and you won't be too far off. Some examples:

Many organizations have a *military* subculture, which might be characterized by having a command-and-control outlook in which the only possible response to an assignment is to get it done, without much discussion, no matter what it takes.

Most also have a *security* subculture – a mindset that sees the world in terms of threats and victims, organizes responses in terms of policies and procedures, and implements those policies and procedures through enforcement rather than consensus.

Another subculture, familiar in information technology groups, consists of *engineers*. An engineer is anyone who sees the world as a collection of problems, all of which can be solved with sufficient ingenuity. Engineers tend to resist or ignore authority and have little patience for members of the security subculture. Both interfere with creative problem-solving.

And so on.

The subculture view can give you some terrific insights about how different individuals are likely to respond. Targeting communications and involvement by subculture, though, won't be possible.

Developing strategies for stakeholder groups

First understand, then plan, then act. That's the philosophy that underlies creation of the stakeholder analysis. The strategies are your plans on how to act toward each individual stakeholder and stakeholder group. They are tailored; that doesn't mean you have to rely on unique ingenuity every time. To get you started, here are some strategies you might find useful:

> *Make it a win:* If possible, as part of the business design process, do everything you can to make the change beneficial for each stakeholder and stakeholder group. If you can't, at least make it as beneficial as possible for high-impact stakeholders. The concept is simple: Make the change as easy to support as you can.

> *Involve:* Involvement is such a workhorse strategy that it gets a chapter of its own. When you successfully involve people, the project stops being something you do to them and starts to be something they own, have contributed to, and take pride in.

> *Promote:* A role-based variant of involvement that increases an individual's impact while providing a tangible and visible reward for providing effective support.

> *Communicate:* Another workhorse that gets its own chapter. The underlying principle is that uncertainty leads to fear, fear leads to anger, and that way lies the dark side ... oh, wait, that's the Jedi principle. Here, the principle is that fear naturally drives resistance, and fear of the unknown is almost always greater than any other fear.

> *Introduce:* Supporting a change can feel lonely and isolating for many employees. Compared to resistance or cynical acceptance, support can have a Pollyanna-ish aura. By introducing supporters to each other and getting them together to compare notes on a regular basis you can reduce their sense of isolation and provide emotional support.

And by making use of ideas that come out of their discussions, you'll help them feel important.

> *Give special treatment:* Some people respond favorably to being singled out for special privileges and perks, or perhaps just one-on-one persuasion that makes them feel more important. In the fictional example that follows you'll see special treatment as part of the strategy for the COO.

> *Defuse:* Sometimes, change resisters are simply frustrated, figuring nobody cares what they have to say about the subject. Giving them a forum for expressing their concerns and acknowledging their legitimacy can, by itself, have a signifi-

cant positive impact.

> *Corner:* Place in a position where overt resistance would be awkward or embarrassing. In the fictional example, this is one of the strategies to be used with the business unit heads.
> *Marginalize:* Sometimes, the best approach is to turn a resister into something of an outcast.

One version of this is social marginalization. It takes subtlety to achieve this without tainting yourself, but it's far from impossible, and can be quite effective.

Another version is positional, sometimes called the *lateral arabesque.* It's a new assignment that isn't a demotion, but does reduce the resister's potential impact.

THE CHANGE/ *A fictional example we'll use throughout this book*

The best way to explain any technique is through examples. As all real-world examples would violate either a non-disclosure agreement, professional ethics, or both, we'll have to use one that's fictional. As the usual disclaimer for fictional works states, any resemblance between the persons and situations described herein and actual human beings and what they have to deal with every day is purely unavoidable.

As best I can, every element in this scenario, including the personality traits and motivations as I describe them, is commonplace.

So here's the situation:

> *The change itself:* Centralizing and unifying a business process that until now has existed in four different versions, developed independently in four business units, all but one of which was acquired between two and five years ago but never integrated into a cohesive enterprise.

To be precise, we'll be centralizing "non-strategic sourcing," also known as purchasing.

> *You:* You're the project manager. You've been with the company for five years. You come from the original, pre-acquisition business unit and spent much of your career as a business analyst. You have a working knowledge of process optimization but aren't a black belt in any of the formal process disciplines.

When the change is finished, you have been promised the role of Purchasing Manager. You aren't sure if this is because the Chief Administrative Officer (CAO) considers you the best-qualified candidate, it's supposed to be a reward for all your hard work, or some minor deity is planning to punish you for some past sins you can't quite recall.

> *Executive sponsor:* The CAO. She has a reputation as an empire builder, but in your interactions she impressed you with her focus on making smart decisions for the business.

> *Additional context:* This project is supposed to be the "pointy end of the spear" for further centralization efforts promised by the CEO to the board of directors as part of his "mandate to achieve the 'synergy targets[2]'" that were built into the business case for making the acquisitions in the first place.

SOME STAKEHOLDERS
CEO

You don't know the CEO well, and the CAO (your executive sponsor) is not part of the CEO's informal inner circle. Here's what you know and can infer: The CEO likes being liked – being popular with employees matters to him.

He isn't a particularly deep, nuanced thinker – he's known for his "ability to simplify complex issues to their essence," which in your experience means he frequently oversimplifies complex challenges and underestimates the effort needed to deal with them … for example, what it takes to integrate acquisitions, as opposed to simply running them as autonomous business units that report into a holding company.

He's also the sort of leader who would rather avoid disruption by smoothing over differences than deal with controversial issues through collaborative problem-solving. It's clear why the integration never happened.

Put all of this evidence together and you rate the CEO a *Supporter* because he has to be to achieve the synergy targets he promised the board. His personal survival depends on it. His Impact rating is *level 3* (high) for obvious reasons.

His status of Supporter is fragile. His preference for avoiding conflict and desire to be liked mean that if the change meets with too many complaints he could easily back away from it, placating the board with some plausible pretext that gives him political cover for his change of mind. That means you need to help him keep his

---

2   Translation: Increased efficiencies that lead to layoff-driven cost reductions.

hands clean with respect to the layoffs that are a required outcome of the change effort. As a practical consequence this means the CAO's signature will be on most communications, not the CEO's.

You figure that to maintain his support you will need to keep him fully informed and will have to get his sign-off on most of the critical decisions to be made during the project (other than the layoffs themselves).

On the other hand, you'll give him the public credit for a generous severance program.

CIO

You've worked with the CIO before and have a pretty good feel for how he thinks and approaches his work. Your assessment isn't particularly positive.

The CIO is nearing retirement. He's never bothered to learn much about post-mainframe information technology and, in conversation, makes frequent, disparaging remarks about personal computers, smartphones, the Internet, any programming language more recent than COBOL, and any methodology more modern than waterfall-oriented structured programming.

Also, while he still shows up and works a "full" 40 hour week, in your opinion he's Retired In Place, leaving all the actual leadership of IT to his direct reports.

He's well-connected in the company, the inevitable result of more than 30 years in various roles. Earlier in his career he apparently was a force to be reckoned with – his name is attached to the original implementations of many of the legacy systems on which the company runs.

He's also mildly sexist, a conclusion you've reached in observing his interactions with his direct reports. He acts as a buddy to the male members of the team, which means everyone except the Director of Application Development, who he does his best to ignore.

In your assessment, she's the strongest member of his team.

You rate him a *resister*, in large part because the CAO has been emphatic that she won't accept IT's waterfall-based development methodologies, which have given IT a company-wide reputation for project failures. Add to that a social factor … the CAO and Director of Application Development are part of an emerging "Old Girl's Network" in the company … and you see no way to get the CIO to be anything other than a barrier.

Because the Director of Application Development will be the point person for the effort and the CIO no longer puts much energy into anything anymore, you rate his impact to be *level 2*: If you tick him off enough he could do some damage, but he can't derail the effort on his own.

Your strategy for the CIO will be to marginalize him, keeping him well-enough informed that he can't complain while relying on the Director of Application Development, to whom he has delegated this responsibility, to keep him out of the important project decisions.

Business unit heads

As former CEOs of independent businesses, you infer the business unit heads are less than delighted at their newly subordinate roles. You know from publicly available material that each of their companies was available for acquisition due to poor financial performance – the result of selling uncompetitive products and poor cost discipline.

So you also infer the business unit heads are better at personal career management than business management. This makes them a triple threat: They have strong political skills, no personal commitment to the company as a whole, and a likely resistance to the change because it will shrink their overall authority.

All three have been vocal in their assertions that everything about their businesses is unique and that changes anywhere will have a damaging ripple effect. You infer they suffer from the "Not Invented Here Syndrome" (NIHS).

Since the acquisitions, performance of these business units has been barely adequate, and the Wall Street analysts have placed a spotlight on this weakness. You infer the business unit heads might be nervous about their continued role in the company.

You also know from publicly available material that, before the acquisitions, each was receiving very generous compensation packages, especially when compared to their performance. So you also infer they will accept business change so long as it benefits them financially.

You put your inferences together and decide:
> With some grumbling, the business unit heads are likely to
   accept the change. Overt resistance might be enough to jeopardize their employment, and because the process in question

Table 1/ Sample stakeholder analysis for process centralization initiative

Stakeholder > Status [3] > Impact [4]	Support/Resistance Factors	Strategy
CEO/ > Supporter > High impact	> His neck is on the line with the board of directors. > Bigger profits mean bigger bonuses. > He likes being liked, so linking him too strongly to any layoffs could turn him into a resister. > But, an implementation that fails to deliver measurable financial benefits will definitely turn him into a resister.	> Keep fully informed. > Engage in critical decisions with formal sign-offs. > Project communications will mostly be under the CAO's signature. > Put his name on a generous severance plan. > Develop clear, well-constructed cost measures in the metrics plan.
CFO/ > Supporter > Medium Impact	> One administrative process instead of four simplifies accounting. > Favorable impact on expenses. > Delays could turn her into an Acceptor. > Will follow CEO's lead if the CEO's support status changes.	> Keep fully informed. > Include accounting changes in project and have her staff own that part of the effort.
CAO (Executive sponsor)/ > Supporter > High impact	> Her oversight responsibility in the current state is a joke. She is theoretically responsible but has no authority over the process to be centralized. > Additional responsibilities and staff will increase her stature in the company. > Sensitive to her reputation as an empire builder – if the buzz in this direction becomes too intense, she might back away from fully supporting the change. > Up to her eyeballs in work already. If her sponsor role requires too much time, this also might cause her to back away.	> Treat as full partner. Keep her fully informed, including the details, and ask her advice on a regular basis. > Focus all communications on the business case, not the organizational change. > Be careful when and how her direct support is used, to minimize the time she needs to spend on the project.
CIO/ > Resister > Medium impact	> A by-the-book waterfall [5]-methodology guy, and the CAO wants all system changes to be implemented using Agile [6] He resents her telling him how to run his department. > IT's reputation for delivery isn't very good, and he's a politician. A successful project could turn him into an acceptor.	> Marginalize: Keep him informed, but don't involve him in project decisions any more than you have to.

3 Supporter, Acceptor, Resister

4 Low impact, Medium impact, High impact

5 In case you aren't familiar with the term, "waterfall" refers to traditional, sequential, big-project requirements/specs/code/test/release methodologies.

6 Another just-in-case-you-don't-know-the-term footnote: Agile is a family of application methodologies characterized by prototyping, iteration, lots of informal interaction with end-users, and many small releases.

Table 1/ Sample stakeholder analysis - Continued

Stakeholder > Status > Impact	Support/Resistance factors	Strategy
Director of Applications Development/ > Supporter > Medium impact	> Her name is on IT's poor reputation for delivery. She sees this project as a chance to improve her reputation. > She has suggested Scrum[7] to the CIO in the past and been rebuffed. Sees this as her chance to make it happen. > The process consolidation means she can retire three systems and a bunch of messy interfaces that absorb significant staff time to support.	> Make sure she gets credit for successful delivery. > Make sure the project plan includes the tasks necessary to decommission the now-unnecessary systems.
Business Unit Heads/ > Acceptors > High impact	> See this project as a reduction in their authority and loss of autonomy. > All three suffer from serious cases of the "Not Invented Here" syndrome. > All three are money-motivated.	> Use a divide-and-conquer strategy, deploy the change one at a time, starting with whomever dislikes the change the least. > Include their protégés/heirs apparent on the design team so it is invented there. > Enlist the CEO's support in establishing a connection between project success and their annual bonuses. > Build into the communications plan, to put them on record as supporting the change.
Business Unit Process Managers/ > Acceptors > Medium impact	> Don't love the change, but don't expect to lose their jobs because of it – expect enough of the new process to be executed in the business units. > Are managers rather than leaders.	> Reinforce that their positions are secure. > Build into the communications plan as a channel, to corner them into taking on leadership responsibilities.
Business Unit Staff/ > Resisters/ > Low impact	> Realistically understand the nature of "synergy targets." > Their loyalty is to the business unit – culturally they've never been integrated into the enterprise. > Can kill the change through malicious obedience[8].	> Communicate business case thoroughly and repeatedly. > Stress the opportunities the project will create (and make sure it creates them, especially for supporters). > Be honest about layoff potential; communicate how the company will take care of those laid off early and often (first choice for open positions elsewhere, generous severance packages, and outplacement assistance).

7 One more methodology definition, just in case: Scrum is a member of the Agile family, better described as a release management methodology than as a development methodology.

8 In case this phrase isn't clear, an example: When my kids were young I once made the mistake of telling them to put on their shoes and socks. That's exactly what they did – they put on their shoes, then they put on their socks.

is administrative, it isn't threatening to their overall authority, at least in the short term. Make it too clear that this is the
first of many centralizations, though, and their status could
easily change to resister.

> You grade their impact to be *level 2*. Their authority over
the process in question is already shared with the CAO, and
with the CEO behind the change they're unlikely to overtly
encourage resistance among others.

> To ensure their continued neutrality, you plan several steps,
such as:

  ▶ Working with the CEO to align their compensation
  with the centralization.

  ▶ Cornering them (see above) by putting them on
  public record as supporting it.

  ▶ Staging the implementation, starting with
  whichever of the three is most supportive, in a
  divide-and-conquer tactic that makes opposition
  increasingly difficult with each success.

These examples should be enough to show you the thought process
to go through in performing a stakeholder analysis. Table 1, while
not complete, provides more examples along with a format for keeping track of your analysis and decisions.

One point that should be clear from Table 1: You should prepare
the stakeholder analysis either entirely by yourself or with a very
small group of people with whom you trust your career. If it isn't
honest, it's worthless. And if it is honest, you won't want it falling
into the wrong hands (defined as "any hands but your own").

It's a terribly sensitive document. Keep it in a private folder.
Encrypt it if you don't trust your sysadmins. If you prepare it in a
group setting, collect everyone's notes at the end of the meeting and
don't distribute meeting notes afterward.

For anything in the Strategy column that leads to assignments,
find ways to present them to the assignees that are logical without
sounding derogatory toward the stakeholders in question.

A WORD TO HIGH-INTEGRITY READERS

By now, you might feel like you need a long shower to feel clean
again – this all might seem sleazy and manipulative.

Depending on your intentions, perhaps this is sleazy and manipulative. Or else it's the exact opposite: An attempt to deal with peo-

ple as individuals, understanding what motivates them so you can adjust both the change itself and how you accomplish it so it minimizes the pain it inflicts.

BUSINESS CHANGE CHECKLIST/ *Stakeholder analysis*
Here's a checklist, to make sure you don't leave anything out. It includes an Assignee column. This provides a typical role for assigning responsibility. Use this to help you understand how to think through who should be assigned responsibility for each task, not as a hard-and-fast answer to the question.

If the reason isn't clear for excluding the champions from the discussions about impact and strategies, it's because these are the highly sensitive discussions that require complete discretion, and no matter how much you trust someone, the more people who know a secret, the less likely you'll be able to keep it.

Table 2/ *Business change checklist*

Responsibility	Assignee	Completed
List affected stakeholders and stakeholder groups	Project Manager, Business Sponsor, Champion(s)	
List factors likely to cause support or resistance for each stakeholder and stakeholder group	Project Manager, Business Sponsor, Champion(s)	
Assess each stakeholder/ stakeholder group's impact	Project Manager, Business Sponsor	
Develop strategies for each stakeholder and stakeholder group	Project Manager, Business Sponsor	

CHAPTER 2/

INVOLVEMENT PLAN

The world, goes the tired old joke, is divided into two kinds of people: Those who divide the world into two kinds of people and those who don't.

Among the kinds of people involved in any business change are perpetrators and victims. You're one of the perpetrators.

What makes someone your victim aren't your foul deeds. It's that your change is happening to them – it's your change, not their change. They have no sense of ownership. If you don't want someone to feel like your victim, that's something you have to provide.

The business change management technique for doing so is known as *involvement*. The plain English word, by a strange coincidence, is also involvement. Go figure.

Bare Bones Project Management covered this subject. Here's what it said:

> *... figure out who, if they aren't with you, are likely to be against you. That list includes, but certainly isn't limited to compliance or internal audit, corporate communications, information security, various managers of various departments likely to be affected by the project in one way or another, and, most important of all, several end-user representatives – if, that is, none are part of the core team.*
>
> *Why do you want to clutter up your project with so many people who won't be performing project tasks? An example illustrates: If you include compliance and information se-*

curity, you can design a secure, auditable system instead of having to retrofit after development is done. It's the difference between a game of pin-the-tail-on-the-donkey, where you try to hit the target while blindfolded, and having, not just open eyes, but guides to help you navigate.

All those other folks in the middle? You have only two choices: Turn them into critics, or into collaborators. If they're collaborators they'll find reasons to like what you're building. If they aren't, they'll do their best to be helpful by putting your work under a microscope to help you find flaws. As one CIO put it, regarding a complainer against the project whom he added to the team, "I would rather have him inside the tent spitting out than outside the tent spitting in on us."

How about those pesky end-users? Isn't it quicker and more fun to develop the system without them, so at the end you can surprise them with the gift of new software?

Well, no. Many methodologies include a formal testing step called End-User Acceptance Testing. All too often it's also called Make Major Changes for No Apparent Reason. End-User Acceptance Testing should take place all the time. Jill the developer should feel comfortable picking up the phone, dialing an extension that's been called so often the numbers have worn off her telephone keypad, and saying, "Hey, Jack, when you have a minute can you drop by? I've made a few changes to the order entry screen and I'd like your reaction to them."

A software project is a pretty big hill. It's better if ... yes, that's right ... Jack and Jill climb the hill together. Regular end-user input keeps projects from going off-course, and provides a strong sense of ownership in the result.

From a project management perspective, involving potential critics can be the difference between on-time completion and a mass of re-do loops. From a business change management perspective, it's the difference between a project that succeeds ... one in which the business changes ... and one that merely completes, after which the project results bounce off the business with no discernable lasting impact.

Your stakeholder analysis tells you who needs to be involved. Your involvement plan guides their involvement.

LEVELS OF INVOLVEMENT

You can involve people in your project at four different levels. They can *perform* tasks, making decisions and recommendations; you can *consult* them, giving them influence over decisions and recommendations; they can have the authority to *approve* work products and recommendations made by other project participants; or you can keep them *informed* of project progress, decisions, and recommendations (with some trepidation, we might as well accept that we'll shorten Perform, Approve, Consult, Inform to PACI).

Here's how they compare:

Perform

Perform means doing the actual work. Once someone does actual work on the project, they become "we" and they own the results of the whole project. Exceptions are rare, so long as you treat all performers with the respect due someone who is helping you achieve what you want to achieve.

And so long as you understand that while you might have authority over core team members, letting you make decisions and make them stick, you have no such authority over the stakeholders you're involving so as to create a sense of ownership.

For the most part, every stakeholder or stakeholder group will perform (or participate in performing) at least one set of project tasks and be given responsibility for the decisions or recommendations that come out of it.

With a few exceptions. For example, when the stakeholder analysis calls for marginalizing a resister, it would be counterproductive to have that resister perform an important task. Since complete exclusion would be both unsubtle and rude, encouraging their overt resistance unnecessarily, you'll usually have to make use of an alternative, such as ***assumed delegation, buddying up,*** or ***harmless involvement.***

WHY NOT RACI?

Involvement plans are usually cast in these terms:

> ***R**esponsible*
> ***A**ccountable*
> ***C**onsulted*
> ***I**nformed*

Working with clients we learned that while they found consulted and informed straightforward, the difference between responsible and accountable was obscure.

Meanwhile, they wanted to know who was going to do the actual work, and also thought that at times, doing the actual work shouldn't automatically lead to having authority to make the final decision.

And so, responsible became "performs," and we replaced accountable with "approves."

Assumed delegation means approaching the individual to be marginalized (marginalizing an entire stakeholder group is rarely a good idea) assuming he/she is too important and busy to become directly involved in the effort. Instead, based on the logic of the organizational chart, you suggest involving a subordinate who is likely to be more congenial.

Buddying up is another alternative. It means pairing the presumed resister with another stakeholder who strongly supports the change; has a forceful personality; and ideally has a lot of political mojo besides. Your supporter will make the resister's participation both official and unimportant.

Harmless involvement means exactly what it says: You find something for the marginalized individual to do that looks important but which won't have much impact on the final result, however it's done or not done.

Approve

First, a word about consensus [9]. Anyone who has had to build one knows the rule: Before you try to bring a group to consensus in a group setting you first bring each member to agreement privately. By the time the group meets, all the dickering should be finished. Time doesn't always allow you to do this. For important decisions, do your best to make the time, as the alternative is an unpredictable result.

Also … just because a group reaches consensus doesn't mean the consensus will be durable enough to withstand the passage of time. Every so often it's a good idea to revisit them, to make sure everyone involved remembers they committed to the idea.

Approve is the most dangerous form of involvement to bestow, for several reasons:

> *It can derail the entire effort:* In change efforts, AND logic applies to approvals: One *yes* isn't a go-ahead, but one *no* kills. So whenever a decision or design has more than one approver, you'll need to go through the hard work of building a consensus.

  Or else, make it clear at the outset that in the absence of consensus, majority rules.

> *It can slow decision-making to a crawl.* The more stake-

---

9   Consensus is often meant to mean everyone agrees with a decision. Don't fall into this trap. Your goal is less ambitious – to get everyone to agree *to* the decision, and support it. This is an entirely different matter.

holders who have to approve a decision, the more stakeholders you have to work with privately first, and the more de-
lay you'll experience before you can schedule a meeting for
reaching the decision.

> *It creates critics.* In the world of business change, approvers
will generally think of themselves as critics. It's the nature
of critics to find flaws, and once they do, they have a reason
to reject whatever it is they're reviewing until the flaws are
fixed.

When the flaws are important, the role of the critic is vi-
tal. When the critic defines personal success in terms of the
number of flaws found, though, you're in trouble: To the critic, no flaws means personal discomfort; found flaws mean a
reason to say no.

Only assign authority to approve when failing to do so
would be a political mistake that could result in serious complaints later on.

> *It can demoralize the performers.* Performers do the real
work. They put their best thinking into their designs. Even
harder, they make compromises so as to reach consensus
with each other.

Then, someone who wasn't part of the discussions, didn't
hear the logic, and didn't participate in the compromises sees
the final result and provides helpful critiques.

Ugh.

You can't entirely prevent this. You can do a lot to reduce the risk by applying the "no surprises" rule to every
Approver. That is: Don't expect anyone to thank you for delivering the final results, all wrapped up with a bow on top,
as a lovely gift to unwrap. It doesn't work that way – doing
this invites criticism, and in fact begs for it.

Keep every Approver up to date, so that by the time
comes to approve the final product they've already approved
everything about it along the way.

Consult

Being *consulted* doesn't provide a full sense of ownership, but it
at least provides a sense of rentership (if that's a word). Consulting
with people involves them without giving them the authority to
sidetrack the effort.

So consult widely. Describe what you're trying to accomplish and ask as many opinions as you can, from whoever might have something important to say. Whether it's because of their responsibility according to the organizational chart, or because of their background and interests, it can't hurt. You never know who might have a useful insight.

Inform

As a general rule, *inform* anyone who might care.

Inform is best treated as an outcome of the Communications Plan (Chapter 7), not as a matter of courtesy. While you'll generally communicate with those who are Informed (according to your involvement plan) before any general announcement, the communication sequence must be according to a carefully crafted plan, not whatever sequence happens to be what occurs to you at the time.

The only situations that might lead you to avoid Informing a stakeholder arise from the marginalize strategy and the assumed delegation tactic. In those cases you might choose to inform via their delegate, who will be in the best position to communicate in the way least likely to trigger actions that could prove awkward.

One more word about Informing stakeholders: Pay special attention to any stakeholder who might be embarrassed by not knowing something about the change. That consideration should be part of how you sequence information delivery.

THE CHANGE (CENTRALIZED PURCHASING)

In Chapter 1 we performed a stakeholder analysis for a fictional change in a fictional company – centralizing the non-strategic sourcing function, also known as purchasing, for a company with four lines of business (original plus three acquisitions). Now it's time to build the involvement plan for this change.

Involvement plans have two parts: A list of key responsibilities and decisions, and their PACI assignments. What follows walks you through creation of the involvement plan for the same business change described in the last chapter.

Key responsibilities

Most project responsibilities will be driven by the needs of the project itself. The seven components of business change management described in this book create some more. And, you might find yourself inventing a few make-work responsibilities, if you find yourself making use of "harmless involvement" (above).

Here are the key responsibilities for our fictional project:

> *Communications:* Communication doesn't happen by itself. It consists of a collection of tasks, to be performed according to a schedule (see Chapter 7 for details).

> *Accounting changes:* As part of centralizing the administrative process you recognize the likelihood that accounting will be affected in some way ... possibly by establishing a charge-back system; very likely with a change to the chart of accounts (see Chapter 4 for more on this subject).

> *Methodology issues:* This project will be the company's first use of Agile. That means there will be a lot of figuring things out as you go along. Someone has to take responsibility for doing the figuring out.

> *Changes to executive compensation:* The stakeholder analysis established the need to link executive compensation, and in particular business-unit-head compensation, to project success. Someone will have to design the details (Chapter 4).

> *Process design:* It's a new process that will replace four existing processes. Someone has to design it, and do so in a way that gains the acceptance of those who will be affected by it.

> *System changes:* It's in the nature of things that modern administrative processes are driven by information technology. While you don't expect centralizing the four existing processes to result in the need for an entirely new system, you do anticipate a need for changes to the one you have.

> *User interface design:* You separate user interface (UI) design from other system changes because doing so will provide an opportunity for increased end-user involvement. After all, the end-users will live in the user interface. Beyond your wanting to involve them to minimize their resistance, they undoubtedly have useful insights to share regarding what works and doesn't work.

> *Facilities redesign:* At this stage of the effort it isn't clear whether the new process will have sufficient impact to require changes to anyone's physical workspace. You include facilities redesign in the involvement plan in case it does (Chapter 4).

> *Metrics design:* Chapter 3 covers the metrics plan. Right now your concerns are: (1) Designing good metrics is always tricky, so you want someone qualified to do the work; (2) the metrics will drive behavior, so you'll need broad buy-in that these are the right ones; and (3) metrics design is a non-trivial task ... it's work, and needs to be performed by someone who commits enough time to do it well.

> *Organizational redesign:* While the nature of this change isn't so large that it's likely to require a major change to the organizational chart, it seems likely that some changes will be needed. Someone needs to design them, along with a transition plan to move everyone into the new organizational structures and reporting relationships (Chapter 4).

> *Training design:* It will be a new process. Nobody will know how to do their jobs the new way unless you explain it to them (Chapter 5).

> *Culture change:* It's an administrative process. How much culture change can it need? Answer: Quite a lot. It's the pointy end of the spear for starting to integrate the previously independent business units, so it's going to call for some changes in attitude on the part of everyone who will have an ongoing role to play (see Chapter 6 for more on this subject).

> *All major decisions:* This is a placeholder, to remind you of both your communications and project governance responsibilities.

> *Critical decisions:* A second placeholder. List critical decisions separately if it will help segment communications and project governance.

> *Escalated issues:* One more placeholder. Like critical decisions, project governance will probably describe escalation mechanisms for issues that can't be resolved at the project-team level.

PACI assignments

Base your PACI (Perform, Approve, Consult, Inform, just in case you've forgotten) assignments on your stakeholder analysis. We'll use the one created in the last chapter to provide some examples. As you read, note that the plan is built around organizational roles, carefully taking into account the individuals in each role.

Which means that if the cast of characters changes, you might need to change your involvement plan.

CFO

The CFO has an impact level of 2, and doesn't really care all that much about this project one way or the other. Even though she is officially a supporter there's no need to ask for much of her time.

So you decide to give her a sense of ownership by selecting a representative to be a performer in the project – ideally a protégé, so you don't have to do much selling to get her final approval on decisions.

And you do need her approval on some key decisions, namely, the accounting changes (of course) and changes to executive compensation.

Business unit heads

According to the stakeholder analysis, you expect the business unit heads to be accepters, but grudging ones who could easily turn into resisters. And with a level 3 impact they can derail the whole process if that happens..

Given their impact you can neither ignore nor marginalize them. Your strategy is to realign compensation so they benefit personally if the change is successful, and to box them in by putting them on record as supporting the change.

Keeping this and their executive standing in mind, your best choice for involving them is to have them assign a member of their staff to participate. In making the request you should emphasize the importance of their assigning someone whose abilities and judgment they trust. "After all," you explain, "it would make no sense to have someone in a meeting who can't speak for you and who has to check back with you every day." You're looking for a protégé, although you don't use that term ... which could be interpreted negatively ... in the conversation.

Everything about this is risky. Involving anyone whose loyalties belong to a potential resister ... especially a covert one ... could result in decision paralysis through endless re-do loops as the participant constantly shuttles back and forth between design "decisions" and design rejection on the part of the executive resister ... in this case a business unit head.

The best you can do is to involve the protégés, discourage them from checking-in too frequently with their boss, and do everything you can to encourage a sense of loyalty to the design team to compete with their sense of loyalty to the business unit head they represent. At some point in the proceedings, if re-dos and other delays become excessive, you might have to discuss the matter with the offending business unit head. Your point: If their representative is doing such a poor job of process design that the business unit head has to frequently override them, that perhaps it's time for the business unit head to become a direct participant.

Also remind the business unit heads that they have final approval once the process design and success metrics have been completed.

What you want, in the end, is for the protégés to sell the acceptability of the process design to the business unit heads, and to box in the business unit heads so they would have to explain the reason for their resistance in a public setting … the sort of setting where it must be couched in terms of potential process breakage (which you can deal with logically), not personal preference.

Final thought on this situation, which mirrors what you'll find yourself dealing with in nearly every business change: You can't accomplish what you need to accomplish through the use of authority … even your executive sponsor is, at best, a peer to the executive resisters.

So you'll have to accomplish it through dexterity.

CIO

You'll remember that in the stakeholder analysis we figured the CIO is a resister, due largely to his comfort with waterfall methodologies and resentment over the CAO's insistence on Agile. We decided to marginalize him, making use of assumed delegation to insulate the change effort from his potential resistance: His impact isn't big enough to derail the change, and keeping the Director of Application Development deeply involved will take care of your political obligations while placing a supporter between you and the CIO.

And in general, the Director of Application Development will want to manage the flow of information to the CIO carefully – not to lie and not to conceal, but to make sure the CIO hears what he needs to hear, explained so as to prevent any possible misunderstanding that might cause him to personally intervene.

Table 3/ Sample involvement plan for process centralization initiative

Decision	CEO	CFO	CAO	CIO	Director, App. Dev	Bus. Unit Heads	Bus. Unit Heads' Protégés	Bus. Unit Process Mgrs	Bus. Unit Staff	App Dev Staff	Accounting Rep	Compliance[1]	Informal Thought Leaders
Communications[11]	I	I	P, A	C [10]	P, A[12]	I	I	P			I		
Accounting changes		A	I			C				I	P	C	
Methodology issues			I		P, A					C			C
Exec comp changes	P[13], A	C, A	C			C							
Process design			A			I	A	P	P	C	C	C	C
System changes				I[14]	A			C	C	P	C	C	
User interface designs						I		I	C	P	C	P	
Facilities redesign			I					A	I	C, A	P		
Metrics design	A	C	A			A	P	P	C	I	P[15], C	C	C
Org redesign	C, A	I	P			I	C[16]	I	C	I	I	I	C
Training design			I			I		I	A	P	P	I	C
Culture changes	C, A	C	P			I	C	C	C	C			C
All major decisions	I	I	I	I	I								
Critical decisions	A	I	A	I	I	I							
Escalated issues			P, A										

Key: P = Perform A = Approve C = Consult I = Inform

10   Compliance includes internal audit, information security, legal, and any other group that establishes internal rules that must be followed.

11   Entries in this row reflect involvement in creating communications. Who receives them once they're created is a different matter.

12   When communications have IT-related content; Consulted is preferable to Approves, given the individual's Resister status and your strategy of marginalization.

13   As a practical matter, the CEO will delegate this, either to HR or to an outside specialist.

14   This "Inform" is part of the CIO's weekly project portfolio status meeting.

15   The Accounting Rep should be fully responsible for financial measures; consulted on the non-financial measures.

16   This is the process-driven organizational redesign to support centralization of the process. The Business Unit Heads are, of course, free to redesign their own organizations however and however often they like.

INVOLVEMENT PLAN

Table 3 shows the full plan. Cross-reference it to the stakeholder analysis in chapter one and it should be self-explanatory.

A few additional comments about it:

Major and critical decisions

Note that nobody has a "Perform" in these rows. That's because the actual decisions will be made in other rows – Accounting Changes, for example. These two rows are placeholders, to make sure you remember the No Surprises Rule – to make sure, that is, that the company's top executives hear everything important from you before they hear another version from anyone else.

And, in this particular project, because of its political sensitivity, the CEO wants final approval for the most critical decisions.

Take a look at the last column – the informal thought leaders. Every company has them. They're the people whose titles don't matter and whose formal roles don't matter very much either. They're the people the executives look to for advice and ideas when they don't feel fully comfortable with a subject.

These folks aren't stakeholders in any meaningful sense of the word, yet their support is important to you. The best way to get it is to involve them informally, which is why their column has a liberal sprinkling of Consults in it.

In case you haven't figured this out: Assume every executive's administrative assistant falls into this category.

Finally, note that the only stakeholders who don't have at least one Perform in their columns are the CFO, CIO and Business Unit Heads, all of whom will Perform through delegation.

Selling the plan

Building the Involvement Plan is easy, assuming you start with a well-thought-out stakeholder analysis.

The hard part is making sure everyone agrees to the kind of involvement you have planned for them.

Exactly how you have each conversation will depend greatly on the different individuals' personalities, and the quality of your relationships with them.

Beyond this, you should also decide carefully who should have each conversation. There will be times when the executive sponsor has to be the one to broach the subject ... for example, when

you've classified the stakeholder as a resister and his or her participation is crucial.

For that matter, there might be times when the executive sponsor
asks the CEO to handle the job.

You also will find situations where you're best off relying on a
member of your team to approach one of their potentially prickly
peers, because they have a good working relationship and you do
not.

A few guidelines:

> Always ask the stakeholder's manager before asking the
stakeholder. You can't assign work to people who don't report
to you. If you try, you're violating the stakeholder's chain of
command, which could cause your whole Involvement Plan
to blow up in your face, and rightly so.

> The exception: Executive-level stakeholders, who will gen-
erally make their own decisions about how they spend their
time.

> When you are asking for representatives from an area, em-
phasize the importance of getting the best, not the ones who
are most easily spared. "Best" in this case means they have
both the qualifications to do the work well, and that their colleagues will trust their judgment.

> It doesn't, however, have to mean the most highly qualified
individuals. First of all, they might be stretched thin already.
And, there's value in involving high potential individuals
who will appreciate a chance to develop and grow.

> Finally, those who will be the most strongly affected by the
chance are often the ones who will do the best job.

> Emphasize the desirability of the manager delegating the au-
thority to make decisions to the representatives. If that isn't
possible, ask for a commitment from the manager that he/she
will turn around decisions quickly, to avoid causing delays
and re-work.

So far as the conversations themselves, your message is straightforward: Your job is to make sure the change is successful. Part of the
change falls into the stakeholder's area of special expertise. You
want to make sure you get the details right. So does the stakeholder,
because he/she will have to live with the result.

One final point: You aren't trying to trick people into accepting
your change through the clever ploy of involving them. If that's your

attitude they'll see right through you … if not when you ask for their participation, then when you disagree and override their opinions whenever they don't come up with your pre-defined solutions.

Your goal is to do everything you can to make the change a collaboration, both to achieve a superior design, and to avoid creating any more victims than necessary.

Executing the plan

You've made the plan, you've sold the plan. Now it's time to execute.

This is another way of saying it's time to build these tasks into the project plan and then to manage the project.

Did I mention I wrote a book that can help you with this?[17]

Table 4/ **Business change checklist – involvement plan**		
Responsibility	Assignee	Completed
Review stakeholder analysis for specific involvement requirements	Project Manager, Business Sponsor	
List major change design decisions and work threads	Project Manager	
Allocate design decisions and work threads (Perform and Approve) to stakeholder groups based on stakeholder analysis and the intrinsic logic of each assignment	Project Manager (Perform); Business Sponsor (Consult and Approve)	
Fill in involvement plan gaps with Consult and Inform indications based on the possibility of interest and expertise	Project Manager	
Incorporate involvement plan assignments and approvals into project plan(s)	Project Manager	

17   *Bare Bones Project Management: What you **can't not** do* (Bob Lewis, 2006).

CHAPTER 3/

METRICS PLAN

Most of what it takes to make change happen in an organization is about people ... understanding them, empathizing with them, persuading them, educating them, and involving them, not necessarily in that order.

Then there's the subject of metrics ... as inhuman a subject as you can find in the world of business.

Nonetheless, without a metrics plan you won't be able to answer the most important question you'll ever be asked about the change for which you're responsible: Was it successful?

With that in mind ...

Somehow or other, we got stuck using *metrics* to mean "How do we know how we're doing?"

Bad word. Bad, bad word. Get down, you bad word, and stop shedding on the sofa.

What this chapter calls, with some reluctance, a metrics plan is in fact a cornerstone of any business change: A clear account of what success will look like, how you'll recognize it when it shows up, and, for that matter, how you'll know when it doesn't.

We need a word that clearly means "how we know how we're doing." Instead we're stuck with *metrics*. Just remember, a metric (or a measure, or a measurement) doesn't have to be a number.

More important, no discussion should ever begin, "What metrics will we use for this?" That should be the second-to-last question you ask [18, 19].

On a more positive note:

THE CORE ASSUMPTION OF BUSINESS METRICS

You get what you measure. That, in fact, is the most important reason to establish measurements of any kind: They drive employee behavior.

It's also why establishing business metrics is risky – do it badly and you'll still get what you measure. Worse, you'll only get what you measure, and if you use the same metrics to assess individual employee performance that you use to measure business performance, employees will do what they can to make the metrics look good, regardless of what's really going on.

In case the point isn't sufficiently clear, include everyone who receives a paycheck, up to and including the CEO, as an employee.

Then look at some prominent corporate failures. There's a very strong chance the unwitting culprit is the Board of Directors' Compensation Committee – the organization that establishes the metrics by which the CEO is assessed.

GOOD METRICS

Chapter 3 of *Keep the Joint Running: A Manifesto for 21st Century Information Technology* (Bob Lewis, 2008) provided a complete account of why metrics are done badly so often, and what's required to establish a useful set of business metrics.

Briefly, any useful set of metrics has six properties … the *6 Cs.* Good metrics are *connected* to important goals; *consistent,* so they always go one way (up, perhaps) when the situation improves and the opposite direction when it deteriorates; *calibrated* so that everyone who measures something gets similar results; *complete,* because anything you don't measure you don't get, which means a system of metrics that isn't complete might cause employees to stop doing important work; *communicated* so everyone knows how the business is performing; and *current* – monitored and modified for ongoing relevance.

---

18 The last question is how you'll collect, analyze, and report the data you'll need to answer the second-to-last question.

19 The first question, in case you're too impatient to wait until we've set the stage, is, "What are you trying to accomplish?"

WHAT TO MEASURE

What you should measure is divided into three levels: Bottom-line improvement, the business outcomes that will drive that improvement, and the improvements to internal effectiveness that make the business outcomes happen. One at a time:

Bottom-line improvement and business outcomes

Successful business change begins with a design and a plan. They define the change that is to take place, and should include some explanation of how the change will make the organization more successful.

The explanation will start by explaining how the change will have a positive impact on one or more of the three *bottom-line fundamental business benefits,* which are to (1) increase revenue, (2) decrease cost, or (3) manage risk better.

The change might directly affect one of these bottom-line benefits, or it might help achieve them indirectly by supporting a larger business strategy that's designed to increase revenue, decrease cost, or manage risk better.

Inside each of these are a surprisingly limited number of options[20]:

Increasing revenue

To increase revenue, companies try to achieve these **business outcomes**:

> Attract new customers.
> Retain existing customers and expand their walletshare.
> Increase sales of existing products.
> Develop new products and services to sell.
> Buy other companies and claim their revenue[21].
> Invest in other companies to take advantage of their ability to make money.

Decreasing cost

Here are the most important **business outcomes** companies use to decrease costs without just being stupid about it:

---

20 This list isn't exhaustive. It puts a pretty good dent in the possibilities, though.

21 As Adam Hartung points out in *Create Marketplace Disruption* (2008), if Company A, with $40 million in revenue, buys Company B with $20 million in revenue and seriously damages it in the process, cutting its revenue in half, Company A will still show $10 million in year-over-year revenue growth as a result.

> Eliminate non-value-adding[22] activities.
> Eliminate non-value-adding steps hidden within value-adding activities.
> Reduce the time and effort needed to execute value-adding steps within value-adding activities.
> Centralize responsibilities executed independently and in parallel in different locations within the business.
> Reduce the number of out-of-specification products (waste) produced by value-adding activities.
> In an extreme crisis, extract wage concessions from employees, from the top executives on down.

These are intelligent ways to cut costs, but far from the only ways. For the sake of completeness, here are some of the more common **business outcomes** companies use to decrease costs that are ... well, there really isn't a better word than "stupid," other than, perhaps, "short-sighted":

> Extract wage concessions from employees in the absence of a crisis, damaging morale ... and, in consequence, productivity and initiative ... in the process. This is especially effective when some of the savings are used to fund executive bonuses.
> Delay filling open positions, thereby forgoing the business benefit that must result from filling the open position (because nobody would fill a position on which the company would take a loss, would they?).
> Cut budgets, leaving it to budget managers to figure out how to get things done anyway. This is a double-whammy – an insult coupled with perverse incentives. It's an insult because it states clearly the assumption that the budget manager's operation is inefficient. It creates perverse incentives because budget managers who successfully pad their budgets will be the ones who end up looking the best.
> Shift costs into the next fiscal year, to make this year look good and this year's bonuses bigger.

Managing risk
Risks describe possibilities of reduced revenue or increased costs. Risks aren't the same as "stochastic" costs or revenue losses – costs

---

22 ConsultantSpeak for "pointless." Anything a business does that has no result customers will care about is a non-value-adding activity.

and revenue losses that occur predictably but randomly.

Employee sick time, for example, is a stochastic cost rather than a risk, because while on any given day you can't predict whether a particular employee will get a cold, with even a hundred employees and a few years of experience you can predict how many employees will be sick on a given day of the year.

That makes employee sick time a cost, not a risk. Compare it to the risk that your biggest customer will go out of business. Even if you have access to its financial records, on any given day it either will or will not enter Chapter 11. All you can do is estimate the probability of the event, estimate the damage if it happens, and decide what to do to deal with the possibility.

Here are the possible *business outcomes* for dealing with risk:

> *Prevent:* Reduce the odds something bad will happen.
> *Mitigate:* Reduce the damage something bad does when it does happen.
> *Insure:* Spread the cost of something bad when it does happen.
> *Hope:* Do nothing about the risk and count on good luck.

Compliance

For the most part, investments in compliance are investments in risk management. One reason: Most of the regulations companies must comply with are designed to reduce risk. Building codes are an excellent example. Second reason: Companies that fail to comply with regulations are at risk of potentially serious fines – a preventable cost.

More about business outcomes

Business outcomes describe the actual change – what you're trying to achieve.

They might revolve around customer satisfaction. They might be an attempt to increase name-recognition. They might be to make your products more appealing to a broader range of potential customers.

For most but not all business outcomes, measuring improvement is straightforward. Demonstrating the connection between successfully achieving a particular business outcome and obtaining the desired bottom-line benefit is, with few exceptions, problematic.

For example, imagine your chosen bottom-line benefit is to increase revenue, and the business outcome you'll achieve to obtain it is to retain existing customers better and expand your share of their wallet. You're going to accomplish this by improving the speed of customer service (cycle time), while making fewer mistakes doing so (quality) and making the customer service experience more pleasant (excellence).

In most businesses, tracking customer retention (repeat business) is a straightforward data mining problem, as is tracking changes in walletshare (change in sales per customer per time interval).

Now ... how do you go about proving the customer service improvements are what led to the improved customer retention and increased walletshare?

The best you can do is show how retention and walletshare change over time before and after the service improvement program launches. This might be convincing, if the company is doing nothing else to improve retention and walletshare at the same time, and the scope and size of the improvements in customer service are large enough to yield a statistically unambiguous result.

Otherwise, you have two choices.

You can choose to adopt only "S.M.A.R.T." goals (specific, measurable, attainable, relevant, and time-bound), ignoring all difficult-to-measure or difficult-to-prove business improvements. The word often used to describe companies like this is "short-lived," because they confuse ease of measurement with importance.

Or, you can do your best to measure what you can, find ingenious ways to gauge effectiveness when you can't, and have confidence in your knowledge of how your business works.

Customer retention is just one example of the challenges of proving that a given business improvement has led to bottom-line results.

As Table 5 shows, the only improvements that are both straightforward to measure and easily proven are new products and services, acquisitions, eliminating non-value-adding activities, and buying insurance.

Improvements to internal effectiveness

You can't directly achieve most business outcomes (buying revenue through acquisitions and insuring against risk are the exceptions). What you do is improve internal effectiveness in some way. That improvement leads to the outcome. Improvements to internal effec-

Table 5/ Improvement tactic measurement

Bottom-line success factor	Typical tactics	Measurability	Provability
Revenue	Attract new customers.	Straightforward	Low
	Retain existing customers and expand their walletshare.	Straightforward	Low
	Increase sales of existing products.	Straightforward	Low
	Develop new products and services to sell.	Straightforward	High
	Buy other companies and claim their revenue	Straightforward	High
Cost	Eliminate non-value-adding activities.	Straightforward	High
	Eliminate non-value-adding steps hidden within value-adding activities.	Difficult	High
	Reduce the time and effort needed to execute value-adding steps within value-adding activities.	Straightforward	Low
	Centralize responsibilities executed independently and in parallel in different locations within the business.	Difficult	Moderate
	Reduce the number of out-of-specification products (waste) produced by value-adding activities.	Straightforward	Low
Risk	Prevent	Difficult	Low
	Mitigate	Difficult	Low
	Insure	Straightforward	High

tiveness are the buttons and levers you can push and pull to make business outcomes happen.

There are only six of these buttons and levers. They are:

> *Fixed costs:* Also known as overhead costs and non-discretionary spending[23], this is what you spend to turn on the lights, before you make any products for customers to buy, and before any customers show up to buy them.

> *Incremental costs:* This is the increase or decrease in costs as a result of processing one more or one less item. Economists, wanting to impress us with their arcane wisdom, call these "incremental costs."

> *Cycle time:* This is the time that elapses between something triggering a process ... perhaps a work order ... and the time the resulting set of steps finish to create the resulting item.

> *Throughput:* Throughput means process capacity – the quantity of output that can be produced in a unit of time.

> *Quality:* The absence of defects, or, conversely, the extent to

---

23 The preferred term among consultants, because it has the most syllables.

which products and services adhere to specifications.

> *Excellence:* The presence of desirable features, ability to customize or tailor outputs to specific needs, and flexibility to adapt to changing circumstances.

If something is being done badly enough you can improve all six of the above parameters, just as the worst process-improvement snake-oil consultants will promise. If, on the other hand, your business processes weren't designed by idiots and aren't being run by more of the same, improvements in some of the parameters will require trade-offs in others. Here's how it usually comes together:

WARNING:

What follows matters, but it's tedious. It's a detailed look at the benefits and trade-offs of each internal improvement and the most common ways of achieving them.

*If you're in the middle of designing a business change, read them now. If not, you might want to skip to the section titled **Metrics plan.***

Fixed costs

The two most common tactics used to reduce fixed costs (other than renegotiating contracts, which doesn't constitute a business change) are eliminating expensive infrastructure and centralizing previously dispersed responsibilities. They have very different dynamics.

Eliminating expensive infrastructure

Fixed costs are the result of investments in infrastructure. It's an investment because it pays a return ... usually, a gain in economic scalability, which means the ability to handle additional volume without incurring much additional cost (Figure 4).

That is, organizations invest in infrastructure to reduce incremental costs, and most of the steps they can take to reduce fixed costs – outsourcing a function, for example – can end up increasing incremental costs.

Centralization

Centralization is a popular way to reduce fixed costs. It does so by consolidating infrastructure and pooling spare capacity, so the organization can take maximum advantage of what it buys. Better, centralization generally avoids the increase in incremental costs that usually accompanies reductions in infrastructure spending. It might even reduce incremental costs, because the organization will gain economies of scale.

Another fringe benefit of centralization is quality, resulting from the increased consistency that comes from doing something one way in high volumes instead of several different ways in lower volumes.

Nothing is free, though, and in the case of centralization what you lose is your ability to achieve excellence. In this case, the loss is of the ability to adapt to the situational needs of each separate busi-

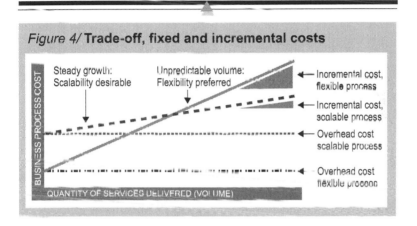

Figure 4/ **Trade-off, fixed and incremental costs**

ness area. Achieving savings through centralization requires standardization – the opposite of customization.

Another common trade-off from centralization is longer cycle times. Like a call center, sometimes you'll get what you want quickly, and sometimes you'll have to wait your turn in a very long queue.

Incremental costs

Incremental costs are the mirror image of fixed costs (Figure 4): Most of the steps organizations take to decrease incremental costs … to improve economic scalability … require investments in infrastructure, which increase fixed costs. If the point isn't clear, compare the incremental cost of processing sales transactions in a supermarket (including the effort needed to connect them to inventory management) with and without bar code scanners. Without them, ringing up and processing each sale takes a lot of expensive manual effort. To get the bar code scanners and systems that make use of the data they generate, supermarkets have to invest significant amounts of capital.

A consequence of investing in infrastructure and achieving low incremental costs: If volume decreases, shedding costs is quite difficult for the simple reason that if incremental costs are low, so are unit savings. The cost line has the same slope whether you're climbing or descending.

Which means that companies that need to be able to shed costs quickly during downturns ... that need *flexibility* with respect to their cost structure ... will want to minimize their fixed costs and will have to accept that as a result, incremental costs might have to increase.

By the way ... just in case the point isn't clear, when companies outsource in order to take advantage of the outsourcer's economies of scale, what's going on under the financial hood is that for pricing purposes the outsourcer is allocating its fixed costs to its incremental costs.

They're still fixed costs to the outsourcer, who has simply been kind enough to convert them to incremental costs for its clients.

Cycle time

For all the attention most process designers give it, cycle time improvements aren't free and aren't accompanied by a lengthy list of benefits. Quite the opposite.

The most important reasons to reduce cycle time are to please customers (most customers value receiving products and services more quickly, and being able to buy your newly released products sooner than those of your competitors) and to improve quality.

Quality improves because defects are only rarely random. Usually they're the result of a production problem, which means if you find one there are plenty more ready to be found as well.

Longer cycle times mean more work in progress, which in turn means more defective work products might be making their way through the system, not to be caught until the final quality check at the end of the line.

If, of course, there's but one quality check and that's where it is.

One more potential benefit is lower fixed costs. It's a benefit that shows up if the mechanism for reducing cycle time is shrinking the inter-step buffers, as this results in less capital being tied up in work-in-progress inventory.

The most common trade-off of improved cycle time is reduced throughput, especially if process designers aren't paying attention. Here's what happens:

To shorten process cycle times, companies have a limited number of options. They can:

> Shorten the cycle time of a single process step.

> Reduce the size of inter-step buffers … work-in-progress inventories … so work spends less time waiting in queues.

> Consolidate process steps so the cycle time of the consolidated step is less than the sum of the cycle times of the steps that were consolidated plus the average queue time between the steps.

If you can achieve any of these with no impact on other process steps, you get nothing but improvement. Usually, you can't.

Shortened step: Often, reducing the cycle time of one process step changes the work that arrives in the next step in some way, for example, by replacing manually transported paper with electronically imaged documents. If a subsequent process step calls for a human being to integrate the information from several separate documents, doing so on a computer monitor will generally take longer than doing so with paper documents a person can spread out on a desk.

If the step that got shorter was a non-bottleneck step, and the step that now takes more time was already a bottleneck, the reduction in cycle time will result in a decrease in throughput.

Smaller queues: Smaller queues are nothing but good – the only impact is that work spends less time sitting and waiting for attention. That's true, at least, until queues become so small that at times the queue empties out entirely. When that happens all downstream steps temporarily grind to a halt, increasing incremental costs and decreasing throughput when they do.

Step consolidation: This is the most dangerous alternative.

Take a close look at Figure 5. At the top is a process optimized for throughput. It's divided into multiple short steps, which means work is pipelined, assembly-line fashion.

The total process cycle time is the sum of the cycle times of the steps: $10 + 12 + 6 + 15 + 10 = 53$ minutes (for simplicity we're ignoring any inter-step work queues).

Step 4 is the bottleneck – the slowest step. Since every other step is faster, the process as a whole delivers completed work at the same pace work exits Step 4 – one item every 15 minutes, or four items per hour.

Compare that to a different process, engineered to produce the same final work product, but with the five steps in the top version consolidated into a single 30 minute step. Since this is the only step, the process cycle time is the same as the step cycle time – 30 min-

---

Figure 5/ Trade-off, fixed and incremental costs

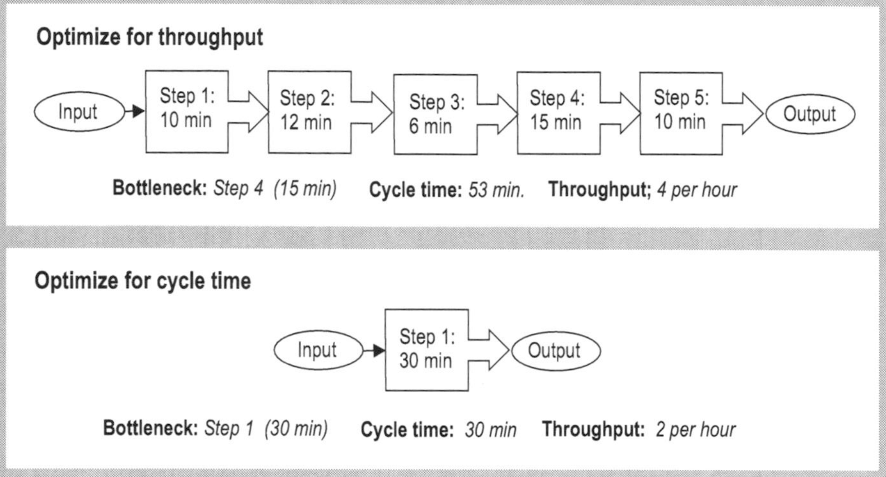

Optimize for throughput

Bottleneck: *Step 4 (15 min)*   Cycle time: *53 min.*   Throughput; *4 per hour*

Optimize for cycle time

Bottleneck: *Step 1 (30 min)*   Cycle time: *30 min*   Throughput: *2 per hour*

---

utes. That's a 23 minute improvement.

Not bad.

Except that the single step is also the bottleneck step (since no other step exists to compete for that honor). Since this version of the process delivers one item every 30 minutes, its throughput measures a leisurely two items per hour – half the throughput of the top version.

This is fine if you care about cycle time and not throughput; not so fine if throughput matters.

Throughput

Improve throughput and you increase process capacity – the process generates more output in the same unit of time. It means you've engineered the process for volume, with the attendant benefit of scalability, which turns into lower incremental costs.

The common consequence of throughput improvement is longer

cycle times. It's the same song as the one sung for cycle time, but played backward.

To understand the specifics, here's what process designers can do to improve throughput:

> Shorten the bottleneck step.
> Add parallel workstations to the bottleneck step.
> Split the bottleneck step into multiple pipelined steps.

Shortened bottleneck step: Since every other step either piles up its output at the bottleneck's input, or can easily keep up with the bottleneck step's outputs as they receive them, it follows that speeding up a bottleneck step will speed up total process throughput ... right up until the bottleneck step is fast enough that another step takes over as the bottleneck. In the top half of Figure 5, speeding up Step 4 to 12 minutes instead of 15 would mean five units of work would exit the process every hour (one every 12 minutes) instead of four.

But speeding up Step 4 beyond that merely shifts the bottleneck to Step 2, because no matter how much faster you make Step 4, it won't matter – Step 3 will only receive a unit of work to chew on every 12 minutes, which means it won't deliver units of work to Step 4 any faster than that.

Parallelism: Now imagine you add a second workstation at Step 4. Assuming there's work to do, each will deliver a unit of work to Step 5 every 15 minutes. With two units of work to chew on arriving every 15 minutes, Step 5 won't be able to keep up ... nor will Steps 1 through 3 be able to deliver work fast enough to keep the two Step 4 workstations busy.

Parallelism can also move the bottleneck. Which means you can, in principle, smooth out the flow entirely by applying the right amount of parallelism to each step so that the total throughputs of all steps are balanced. In this case it would mean 10 workstations at Step 1, 12 at Step 2, 6 at Step 3, 15 at Step 4, and 10 at Step 5. This yields a throughput of 60 per hour at each step, balancing the process so there are no bottlenecks. Sadly, it might also result in serious over-capacity if customer demand isn't up to the challenge.

Splitting a bottleneck step: Splitting a bottleneck is the exact opposite of consolidating steps, and has the opposite effect: It both moves the bottleneck to a different step, thereby increasing throughput, and it almost certainly increases cycle time ... it's rare that a process designer can split up a step so efficiently that no additional handling time is needed.

Quality

Quality, if you believe the book title[24], is free. Actually, it isn't. What quality generally does is pay for the investment required to get it – a very different matter.

Organizations that improve quality by reducing the sources of variation … by reducing the number of defects instead of catching more of them … also reduce incremental costs, because the cost of waste has to be allocated to the cost of sellable items.

Organizations that improve quality by increasing the level of inspection raise incremental costs, of course, as the cost of the inspections has to be allocated to the units.

Nor is this necessarily the wrong answer, because …

Achieved intelligently, improvements in quality have only one trade-off – reduced excellence.

Quality is the absence of defects. Many long books (and some annoying short ones) have been written on this subject. For our purposes, to improve quality organizations can either:

> Reduce the sources of variation in each process step, or …
> Reduce inter-step work buffers, so systemic errors are caught after fewer defective products have been made, or …
> Increase inspections at the end of the process.

Increasing inspections will improve customer satisfaction in that the company is less likely to ship defective products. According to the experts in this subject, everything else about increasing inspections is supposed to be bad, because instead of fixing the problems that cause defects the organization chooses to ignore them.

This is sometimes the case. But not always. Some organizations live and die on excellence – their ability to deliver customized products and services to their customers. Since customization is the opposite of standardization, it's also the opposite of reducing the sources of variation in each process step. By definition, customization means doing something different every time.

If you want to preserve quality under these conditions, there's nothing for it but to increase the time and effort spent in inspections.

Excellence

The biggest fringe benefit that comes from excellence is revenue. Companies can sell excellent products at higher prices, and usually

---

24   *Quality is Free*, Philip Crosby, 1980.

at higher margins as well.

Adding excellence generally makes achieving quality harder, for all the reasons stated above. Even when excellence doesn't mean customization … when it's mass-produced excellence, as in luxury automobiles … excellent products are generally more complicated than less-excellent ones. Sometimes they include more fragile materials, too.

METRICS PLAN

If you've gone through the thought process described in this chapter as part of the process of designing the business change you're responsible for, developing the metrics plan will be, if not easy, straightforward. If you haven't, it's what you have to do next because this three-layer account of the business change is the first component of your metrics plan.

A word of warning, or maybe encouragement: Metrics are something every business executive wants, right until they find out what will be required to get them. The data-collection required for useful metrics isn't expensive, if it's built into the business process or practice – that isn't the

PERFORMANCE METRICS VS SERVICE LEVELS

A fundamental decision when establishing metrics is whether to measure performance or service levels. The difference:

Performance tells you how you're doing, generally as the mean and standard deviation of whatever it is you're supposed to accomplish. Use performance measures when your want to continuously improve with respect to this specific performance parameter.

For example, you might decide to measure cycle time performance because customers value quick delivery, and will value quicker delivery even more.

Service levels define the minimum acceptable level of performance, and how often you achieve it. Use service level metrics when failing to achieve some level of performance will cause problems, but additional improvement won't result in business benefit.

You might, for example, know your process will have to handle between 3,000 and 4,000 transactions each month. Once throughput reaches that level, no additional improvement matters.

Note that by deciding to use a service level measure you're actually applying a quality metric to one of the other process performance parameters – you've defined the target specification for that parameter, and will measure how often you're out of spec.

issue (assuming the new process design includes data collection; otherwise it's a big issue and you need to fix it).

Very often a part of the problem a business change is intended to solve is not having metrics. You have no baseline against which to measure improvement, and no data collection mechanisms built into the current way of doing things.

It's your change. You've committed to making it happen, which means your name is on the promised improvements.

If you manage the current operation, the absence of reliable metrics is something that's within your authority to fix. Fix it.

Otherwise, it's time to apply one of the iron-clad rules of scope management: Nothing is free. Your job is to improve things, which includes establishing metrics for the future state. If you're to also establish the baseline, insist on the time, budget and authority to get it.

Discuss this with the business sponsor before starting any change effort, because by the time you start implementing a new way of doing things it will be too late to do anything about it.

But … what are you to measure?

Component #1: Business improvement goals

Your business improvement goals consist of the bottom-line benefit you plan to achieve, the business outcomes that will make the bottom-line benefit happen, and the internal improvements to effectiveness that will drive the business outcomes.

Carrying forward the business change example we used for the stakeholder analysis and involvement plan (Centralized Purchasing):

Bottom line benefit: Reduce operating costs and reduce the risk of inaccurate financial reporting.

Business outcome: Centralizing an administrative process currently undertaken separately by each business unit.

Improvements in internal effectiveness: Lower fixed costs, reduced incremental costs, and improved quality.

These are the goals. State them in English, not as numbers.
Yet.

Component #2: Business improvement metrics

Okay, it's time. Time to decide what raw data you'll need and what computations you'll perform using it. It's also time to decide how solidly you're going to establish the causal relationship between the change you're trying to institute and bottom-line business benefit.

The minimum

Your metrics plan must include metrics for the planned improvements to internal effectiveness. It also includes your decision as to whether to use performance metrics or service level metrics (see sidebar).

Fixed and incremental cost metrics

Fully delegate responsibility for designing these to Accounting. We already made this decision in Chapter 2, and anyway, this is Accounting's job. They're the professionals – leave it to them.

Cycle time

Cycle time measurement is simple in a discrete processing environment[25]. Each item, whether it's a car to be built or an insurance policy to be underwritten, enters the system at a definable moment and exits the system at another definable moment. Subtract, record the instance in a database, and you're done.

That works so long as the items being processed are individually identifiable. If they aren't, and the process includes work-in-progress buffers to which indistinguishable items will be added on one side and pulled at random from the other, you'll have more work to do to figure out how long, on the average, an item stays in each work-in-progress buffer.

Measuring cycle time in flow environments[26] is more interesting. If the flow is linear it isn't too bad – measure velocity in the pipes (real or metaphorical) and the computation is straightforward.

If the flow environments includes any mixing stages, where fluid (real or metaphorical) is accumulated from multiple sources, and over time from each source, measuring cycle time can get interesting.

This discussion assumes you're dealing with a mass-production environment – a process that handles lots of copies of similar items. That isn't always the case.

Take software development. Not all objects, services, modules, or other units of software are created equal. Either weight each item by the estimated degree of difficulty or measure cycle time for each difficulty level separately.

Every measurement situation presents its own challenges. These

---

25 "Discrete" as in "produces countable items," not "discreet" as in "you can trust it with secrets."
26 Anything that produces a continuous flow of gas, liquid, pellets, grains, or goo is a flow environment.

are included to provide a hint of what you're in for. Beyond that, the solutions are, as the textbooks say, left as an exercise for the reader.

Throughput

Compared to cycle time, measuring throughput is almost always straightforward. In discrete environments, count how many items exit the process in a unit of time. In flow environments weigh how much stuff comes out in a unit of time.

Quality

In order to measure quality you have to have specifications and a way to determine whether the process outputs adhere to them.

Measuring quality is easier with mass-produced items. Take random samples, compare their characteristics to the specs, and you're good to go.

Software lies at the other extreme, as your teams will only program each object, service or module once. It's worse: Your knowledge is only as good as your test plan, which means you never know how many defects a software module contains – only the defects you were able to spot.

One more challenge that isn't unique to software: You have to decide whether to use black-box measures, white-box measures, or both.

Black box measures ignore how well something is built – all that matters is how it behaves. White box measures look at how items are constructed as well. Software illustrates the point well: Black box measures count bugs. Code reviews, to determine whether the developer adhered to style and architecture standards, are white box measures.

Excellence

Quality is what customers notice when it isn't there. Excellence is what they notice when it is there.

Excellence, more than any other dimension of internal effectiveness, is intrinsically difficult to gauge, and almost impossible to gauge objectively. It's the luxurious sensation of Italian leather, the nose, flavor and finish of a fine wine, the sense of astonishment when admiring fine art.

How do you measure excellence? It depends on the specifics of your situation. Customer/user surveys are popular, if unreliable.

Consumer products companies hire panels whose tastes reflect those of their customer bases. Marketing professionals make use of focus groups.

Do your best. Just make sure the people you'll need to convince when your change is in place agree that your data will be acceptable.

The Change (Centralized purchasing)

In our centralized purchasing example we need to measure fixed costs, incremental costs, and the defect rate. In its current form, none of the business units measure process costs or quality problems (transactions that can't be processed until a human being makes a bunch of phone calls to track down what's really going on).

You confer with the business sponsor (the CAO) and Accounting to put a game plan together. After quite a bit of skull-scratching you agree there's no practical way to develop a reasonable estimate of current-state fixed costs. Accounting will undertake a study to provide an acceptable baseline estimate of incremental costs on a business unit by business unit basis.

You'll take the lead in a quality study, which you'll perform by asking all involved in processing transactions to keep a log of the total number they process and the number that need special handling.

For a month. You figure that if you ask anything beyond this the quality of the data you receive will decline rapidly as everyone involved loses interest.

So far as the quality metric itself, you look at the nature of the transactions being handled. They are purchase orders, and have both header and detail information. Were you to classify each transaction as accurate or inaccurate you'd lump together transactions with one line-item in the detail and transactions with dozens of line items.

So instead you define two metrics: The transaction header defect rate and line-item defect rate. For both you'll use performance metrics – mean and standard deviation – because every increment in improvement provides additional business benefit.

With the CAO's approval you also decide that going beyond this to divide defects into categories to support further analysis would be overkill.

Beyond the minimum

You have two choices when it comes to determining whether a business change has accomplished its goals. You can take it on faith that if you achieve the planned improvements to internal effectiveness then good things will happen.

Or you can try to measure the good things, and demonstrate the chain of causation connecting internal effectiveness to them.

Sometimes you can, sometimes you can't.

Imagine the proposed change is supposed to lower costs. The change will improve process efficiency; the plan is for the cost reduction to fall to the bottom line by laying off the excess staff.

Under these circumstances you can and should measure the actual reduction in cost – easily done by adding up the total compensation of the departed employees, netted against the cost of their severance packages.

Now imagine the same proposed change, but in a company that's experiencing steady sales growth. Different plan: With the improved process the company should be able to increase the number of employees more slowly than would be the case if it left the process alone.

Measuring slower hiring is a more interesting challenge. It's possible ... you can use sales volumes and hiring patterns for past years to get a handle on the situation. But it's more difficult, and the situation is further complicated by how human beings react in this sort of situation. The managers in charge knows they're supposed to hire more slowly, and so they will, even if the new process isn't panning out as well as hoped and the existing staff is dreadfully overworked as a result.

The Change (Centralized purchasing)

For our example, "measuring" the business outcome is easy. Either the new, centralized process is in place handling all transactions or it isn't.

As for the bottom-line benefits, you, Accounting and the CAO decide to shrug insofar as any improvement in labor costs. Centralizing the process will free up staff in the business units. Since it's up to each business unit head to decide whether to lay off or redeploy the staff that used to be responsible, you agree there's no practical way to find these cost savings.

On the other hand, by centralizing purchasing you expect to be able to negotiate with vendors more effectively, netting better prices for the products the company buys on a regular basis. Comparing what the company actually spends with what it would have spent for the same items using historical purchase prices is entirely feasible.

You build that analysis into the project plan and system design.

As for risk reduction, that's never overtly measurable. Inaccurate financial reporting either does or doesn't happen. It hadn't happened before the change, even though the risk appeared to be fairly high based on how the different business units handled things.

That being the case, you have no practical way to know the risk has been reduced.

Component #3: Targets

In some but not all cases you'll want to go beyond defining metrics that will let you assess the extent to which the business has improved – you'll want to establish improvement targets.

Defining targets can be a mixed blessing. On one hand, with targets in hand you will be in a better position to determine whether the design is good enough to implement or not.

On the other hand, with targets in hand, the operational manager responsible for overseeing the work once the change has been put into place has a clear statement of how much improvement is good enough. Once the target has been reached, there's less reason to continue improving.

The Change (Centralized purchasing)
Given the limited accuracy you expect of the baseline measures you and Accounting will be developing, you decide setting improvement targets would be a bad idea.

Component #4: Reporting system

Defining a metric is one thing. Getting the actual numbers is another matter entirely. To get the numbers you need to build data collection into the process flow, build the means for recording the collected data into the same information system that will be used to support the work, and develop reporting programs so you actually get the information.

Component #5: Metrics parsimony

Go back to the six Cs that are the criteria for any system of metrics that does more good than harm. One of the Cs is *complete* – the consequence of understanding that anything you don't measure you don't get, no matter how important it is.

Especially if you aren't certain of the factors that drive business success you might be tempted to measure everything that might matter. Or, you might be tempted to organize your metrics into a flat list of stuff that, by telling everybody everything, enlightens nobody about anything.

Be parsimonious in deciding which metrics to define, collect data for, and present. Organize them into a hierarchy of presentation so at any one time you present a clear picture instead of a profusion of numbers.

IN CONCLUSION

A metrics plan isn't as much work as it might seem after having read this chapter. Most of the work should have been done as part of designing the business change – the bottom-line goals, business outcomes and improvements to internal effectiveness should be in place and clearly stated. So you should be able to start this process with the first metrics plan component already in place.

That leaves you to turn the goals into metrics, possibly to establish targets, and design the reporting system.

And, once you've instituted the change, to use the system to determine whether or not you're making progress.

One more thing: If your metrics show you aren't making progress, don't make a mistake I've seen even professional process consultants make, which is to decide you settled on the wrong metric. If you did, it means you set the wrong goals.

Leave your metric alone and figure it's telling you something important. Find out why the business change isn't delivering its intended results and *fix the problem.*

That's why you have a metrics plan in the first place.

Table 6/ Business change checklist – Metrics

Responsibility	Assignee	Completed
Determine expected bottom-line benefits: Revenue, cost, and/or risk.	Business Sponsor	
Define business outcomes expected to yield the bottom-line benefits.	Business Sponsor	
Rank internal effectiveness parameters (fixed cost, incremental cost, cycle time, throughput, quality, excellence) in order of impact on business outcomes.	Business Sponsor, Change Design Team	
Design metrics to gauge improvement in the key internal effectiveness parameters.	Business Sponsor, Project Manager or delegate	
Design metrics to gauge delivery of business outcomes (and, optionally, to demonstrate the connection between internal effectiveness improvements and the business outcomes).	Business Sponsor, Project Manager or delegate	
Optional: Develop analytics to demonstrate connection between business outcomes and bottom-line benefits.	Business Sponsor, Project Manager or delegate	
Optional: Establish targets for one or more metrics.	Business Sponsor	
Design system enhancements to support metrics reporting and add to the system specifications.	Project Manager or delegate	
Perform final metrics plan review for proper balance between parsimony and completeness.	Business Sponsor and Project Manager	

CHAPTER 4/

STRUCTURE PLAN

Most unanticipated consequences are anticipatable[27].

Unanticipated consequences aren't usually the result of systems being so complex that any change yields chaotic, unpredictable outcomes. More often they're the result of ignorance (including willful ignorance), bad logic, a focus on short-term interests, ideological blinders, or more than one in combination.

Most often, that is, unanticipated consequences come from failing or refusing to think things through.

A wide variety of structures and systems in the organization will have, over time, converged and adjusted to stabilize the organization in its current configuration. Fail to change them to stabilize the configuration you're trying to achieve and your planned change will slide off the organization as if it were Teflon coated.

It's an easily anticipated consequence that far too often isn't.

A METAPHOR TO ILLUSTRATE THE POINT

Instead of planning an organizational change, we're going to change an organism. We've been hired by the Society of White Tailed Deer (SWTD). Its members are sick and tired of being prey animals. They've decided to become predators, leaving some other species to deal with their traditional enemy, the Venison Lovers of America (VLOA).

---

27 For example, "The Unanticipated Consequences of Purposive Social Action," Robert K. Merton, American Sociological Review, Vol. 1, No. 6 (Dec., 1936), pp. 894-904/

We assess the situation and perform a root cause analysis, as all good consultants do. The problem, we conclude, is that the deer have the wrong teeth. Their dentition is just fine for chewing plant matter, but is all wrong for catching and killing squirrels (the deer have always found squirrels annoying, and figure this is their chance for some payback).

And so, at considerable expense (we are, after all, consultants), the deer undergo genetic engineering and end up with longer, pointier teeth to replace the flat grinding ones that had evolved over the millennia.

Sadly, the change is a failure. The deer, in spite of their new and more impressive teeth, can't seem to catch any squirrels, or anything else for that matter, other than the same old plants, which they can no longer chew.

We explain to the deer that the problem is that they are resistant to change … perfectly natural, but still a big issue. So we give them copies of our new book, *Who Moved My Squirrel,* while promising to find a way to increase buy-in to the new behaviors they need to exhibit in order to be successful.

Analyzing the situation more deeply we discover a new root cause. The eyes of the SWTD's members are on opposite sides of their head. They provide a 360 degree view of the landscape, but no binocular vision. Their vision is perfectly optimized for detecting predators, but nearly useless for homing in on squirrels.

A selective breeding program quickly[28] fixes this problem, and the deer go squirrel hunting, and more importantly, squirrel catching[29].

At which point yet another problem turns up – their digestive tracts are optimized for a diet of plant matter. Squirrel meat causes incapacitating indigestion.

By now, I trust the point is clear: Deer are optimized to be plant-eaters in any number of ways. Change just one feature and you don't end up with a successful organism. You end up with a mess, and going back to the way things were is far easier than continuing to move forward.

Which is why even the most rapid evolutionary change happens slowly, in small increments, over millennia: All systems have to keep up.

---

28 137 years.
29 It's a sight to behold.

BACK TO THE POINT

You don't have millennia. You have months. The more significant the change, the more every structural element in the company is likely to be lined up against it.

That being the case, it's up to you to make sure all of your organization's structural elements are modified in tandem with the change you're leading so they reinforce it instead of blocking it.

Fortunately for you, organizations aren't as complicated as organisms, and even more fortunately for you, you have a brain. This chapter shows you how to use it to plan changes to the organizational structure – the changes that will push the organization in the right direction instead of causing it to snap back to its original shape just as soon as you stop pushing.

Structure is how the organization is put together. It includes:

> *How to organize:* It's the dreaded organizational chart. If it isn't consistent with the change you're trying to put into place, it will prevent the change from taking place. A good one starts with a clear organizing strategy, then plans the specific reporting relationships. To define these terms:

> ► *Organizing strategy:* The principles that underlie the design of the organization – the major categories of work that define the responsibilities of its top layers.

> ► *Reporting relationships:* Who reports to whom and how responsibilities are partitioned … the organizational chart itself.

> *Facilities:* The physical nature of the workplace what each office or cubicle is like, who sits near whom, which departments and workgroups are in proximity.

> *Governance:* How the organization makes decisions – both the official process and the informal ones that precede it and surround it.

> *Accounting:* The basic accounting system is neutral to most changes. Likewise the chart of accounts. Modifying these to accommodate a business change is a mechanical problem. Failing to change who owns which expenses and revenue, on the other hand, or changing them inappropriately, can entirely block a change.

> *Compensation:* What behaviors, attitudes, skills, and intangibles the company values as expressed by its loudest form

of communication … paychecks and bonuses; what is often called "incentives."

Over time, these tend to smooth out, mesh, and grow together. They reinforce each other, so that when one gets out of whack, the rest keep the organization on course while exerting pressure on the out-of-whack element to get back into whack.

So while it isn't true that "most employees resist change," organizational structure ensures the organization as a whole will tend to remain in a stable configuration, whether or not that stability is appropriate to changing circumstances or not.

Which means it's up to you to figure out which elements of the organizational structure have to be modified, and how, so they reinforce the change you're trying to make instead of the status quo.

One at a time:

HOW TO ORGANIZE

In the end, everyone needs to know who they report to, and everyone needs a clear understanding of what their part of the organization is supposed to do. Beyond this, minimizing the gray areas where two different managers or executives both are accountable for the same responsibility is a worthwhile goal, as is the complementary goal of minimizing the number of responsibilities for which everyone can plausibly deny accountability.

To achieve all of this, start with a clear organizing strategy, then decide on the specific reporting relationships.

Organizing strategy

Never mind the specific organizational chart. That comes later, or should. Organizational design starts with a decision – what organizing principle or principles to use when dividing responsibilities. Among the most popular are:

> **Product:** Specific products or product categories. *Line of business* is a synonym.
> **Customer:** Dividing responsibilities by customer segments. There are several ways to go about this, for example:
  ▶ Geographically: By continent, country or region.
  ▶ Size: Major accounts vs small business vs consumer customers.
  ▶ Demographic: Men vs women; Caucasian vs African-American vs Asian vs Hispanic/Latino; Boomer vs

Yuppie vs Gen X vs Millennials.

▶ Sector: For-profit businesses, non-profits and government agencies are common examples; each require different selling and servicing strategies.

> *Channel:* The most common are retail stores, catalog, e-commerce (Web), and direct sales.

> *Function:* Type of work – Design, Manufacturing, Supply Chain, Marketing, Finance/Accounting, Human Resources and so on.

How to organize, in four steps

With the exception of business functions, all of the other ways to organize face the market in one way or another. This is why the *first step* of organizational design is to either organize according to just one of these strategies, or to organize as a hybrid, with some responsibilities assigned functionally and the rest assigned according to exactly one market-facing principle (and if the market-facing organizing principle is by customer, choosing just one of the customer segmentation alternatives).

It scarcely needs to be said that your choice should be guided by the fundamental strategy of the business. From your perspective, trying to implement a specific change, what matters is that following this rule helps prevent the political infighting that is otherwise inevitable as the responsibilities of organizational peers collide.

Trying to make this happen can be frustrating, because those responsible for organizational design usually see validity to all of the organizing principles, all at once. Trying to organize according to all of the valid perspectives, though, creates an organizational platypus – something that looks like a duck from one angle and a beaver from

WARNING! A REORGANIZATION IS NOT A CHANGE

Far too often, business leaders reorganize (or realign) without any plan to change how work gets done. The reorganization (or realignment) is the change.

Don't do this. The only change that's of any value in an organization is a change to how work is done – that should be self-evident, because if the way work is done doesn't change, nothing about the organization's products and services will change ...

Which means nothing visible to customers will change ...

Which means nothing has changed.

Other than having inflicted significant cost and disruption on employees, who will unavoidably pass it along to customers in some way, shape or form.

Which means something has changed after all.

Just not in a good way.

another, while laying eggs and inflicting a venomous bite[30].
Instead, define the lower layers within the larger layers according to the remaining organizing principles. It's entirely valid, for example, to organize by line of business and within each line of business to organize by geography.

Here's the **second step**: Except in the case of purely functional organizations, describe the areas that have functional responsibilities as shared services. Each will be responsible (and have commensurate authority) for establishing standards and policies for their areas of responsibility (examples: marketing "owns" the brand; IT defines technology standards; HR administers personnel policies and procedures, and so on). Describing them as shared services will help emphasize that supporting the market-facing groups comes first; enforcing their authority comes after and is a poor second-best to establishing collaborative relationships.

OWNERSHIP VS STEWARDSHIP

The term "ownership," while common, is regrettable, because as is always true with metaphors, those who use them carry them off a cliff.

When you assign a responsibility for some corporate asset, process, or anything else, use the term steward *instead of* owner. *Owners say (and think) "It's mine!" Stewards take care of something for someone else.*

Far better perspective in every respect.

The **third step** is a decision: What level contains the "unit of optimization."

One of the most important laws of design, whether you're putting together an aircraft or a business, is that in order to optimize the whole you have to sub-optimize the parts[31]. Most often, the enterprise as a whole is the unit of optimization, and each division within it has to make trade-offs … sub-optimizations … to make the enterprise as a whole as effective as possible.

There are times, though, when this is the wrong answer. Sometimes the right answer is to organize as a holding company, that allows each line of business to optimize itself without having to take into account the impact on the other lines.

Making this decision clearly can save a great deal of aggravation, especially for businesses that grow through mergers and acquisitions rather than organically. If the unit of optimization is the enterprise, part of the M&A process is integrating the new business unit as quickly as possible, replacing whichever systems and pro-

---

30 Don't push this metaphor too far – it isn't worth it. I just like platypuses (or is that platypi?).
31 *Keep the Joint Running: A Manifesto for 21st Century Information Technology,* Bob Lewis (2008)

cesses are redundant with their enterprise equivalents.

If the unit of optimization is the line of business ... the business unit ... then little or nothing is centralized, other than what might be required for accounting and compliance purposes.

There's one exception when applying these three steps, and it ends up validating them: In some cases the best way for a company to try something new is to incubate it in a mostly-independent sub-business, even if the enterprise isn't otherwise organized as a holding company. This is how many retailers got started in e-commerce, for example – they might have been organized functionally or by region, but they created a separate e-commerce department to build out a Web presence. Once they were firmly established on the Internet, they then re-integrated e-commerce responsibilities back into the enterprise.

If the new venture is sufficiently different from the core business it sometimes makes sense to spin it off as a wholly independent company. Clayton Christensen's description of how two companies – S. S. Kresge and F. W. Woolworth – entered discount retailing[32] demonstrates the point particularly well. The story:

A FEW WORDS ABOUT OPTIMIZATION

The word "optimize" has been abused so much that a few more words about it are in order.

First of all: While it's frequently used as a euphemism for "cut costs," that's a very bad usage. Optimizing something is an alternative to minimizing (or maximizing) it, not a synonym.

Second: Optimization is only meaningful with respect to one or more stated variables. Cost is certainly two of them (fixed and unit). There are four more, covered in detail in Chapter 3.

Deciding which level of the organization should be the unit of optimization means, in part, that whoever is responsible for that level decides which of the six variables to optimize for.

Kresge spun off its discount retailing venture into a separate entity (K-Mart). Woolworth's made the opposite choice with its competing venture, Woolco.

For both companies, their new discount retailing experiment constituted a new channel. For both, organizing according to channel undoubtedly conflicted with their organizing strategy (most probably a product/shared-services hybrid).

By managing K-Mart as an independent business unit, Kresge let it figure out what it needed to do to succeed without subjecting it to all the structural forces that would have pressured it to conform

---

32 *The Innovator's Dilemma* (1997)

to the S. S. Kresge store model … the exact mold K-Mart had been created to break out of.

By failing to separate Woolco from its existing organization, Woolworth created conflict in everything Woolco needed to do, from merchandising to marketing to finance and beyond. No matter what the subject, the responsibility belonged separately to two different executives with entirely different requirements.

Woolco bounced off the existing Woolworth organization and died. It never had a chance.

There's one more step, which is necessary unless you're the person in charge of the organization. This *fourth step of organizational design* is to recommend, and more important, how to recommend.

Not every executive has the patience to deal with this whole thought process. For many, organizational design consists of throwing responsibilities at the wall to see how they stick and how they clump.

Others decide based on who they prefer to have reporting to them directly … who they like better and trust more … and allocating responsibilities depending on what each is good at. (Don't, by the way, sneeze at the thought process behind this approach. Trusting your management team matters a lot.)

And some approach the subject intuitively rather than analytically, drawing boxes and shuffling them around until they end up with something that looks workable – not necessarily bad, but probably inconsistent and driven in part by their mood and current complaints.

If you're dealing with a decision-maker who lacks patience with the thinking process outlined here, lay out a few alternatives based on different organizing principles and present them as starting points. As the two of you fiddle with them, don't talk about organizing principles. Just highlight where excessively hybrid approaches will lead to conflicting responsibilities.

In the end, no organizational design is ever perfect. Do your best to shape one that's workable and move on.

The Change (Centralized purchasing)

In our test case, the company is organized as a product/shared-services hybrid, and is part-way between the holding company model and one of enterprise-level optimization. The lines of business … the result, you'll recall, of a series of acquisitions … are each responsible for different product lines and are jealous of their autonomy. Centralized responsibilities like IT, Finance/Accounting, and Human Resources are shared services; their directors tend to emphasize control over service.

In the long run this attempt to split the difference is unhealthy, creating conflict without providing much in the way of offsetting benefit. The current change, in fact, is the pointy end of the centralization spear ... the CEO's starting point for resolving the matter in favor of a more integrated enterprise.

Which is all good news for our planned change. While it moves the enterprise in the right direction, it doesn't violate the existing world order. By centralizing Purchasing, a responsibility that previously belonged to the lines of business, it re-constitutes it as a shared-services responsibility. While newly centralized, the CAO's responsibility in running it is to support the existing lines of business, which will otherwise continue to operate very much as they're accustomed to operating.

PROCESS VS PRACTICE (VS INVENTION)

When there's work to be done, organizations have three ways of going about it.

Processes *are defined sequences of steps which, when followed reliably, result in repeatable, predictable results. Those who design processes extract the need for knowledge from those who perform roles in it, moving their expertise into the process itself – key to making the process repeatable. Processes are recipes. Follow the steps and you get the right results.*

Practices*, like processes, are defined collection of steps that lead to desired results. Unlike process, in a practice the steps are not necessarily sequential, nor is it possible ... or desirable ... to move knowledge out of the heads of the practitioners and into the series of steps themselves.*

Practices depend on the skill, expertise, and judgment of the practitioner. They are the best choice for situations that have a lot of variability, and especially a lot of unpredictable variability.

Invention is what organizations do when they face a situation for the first time and haven't yet established a process or practice. If there's no intent to establish a process or practice, improvisation is a more accurate term.

These are, by the way, poles in a continuum, not independent categories. While some work is more process-line and other work more practice-like, most work will have some characteristics of both, along with a dash of invention to keep things interesting.

Reporting relationships

With a clear organizing strategy you're in a position to design an organization that can work. You're positioned for success – at the starting gate, not the finish line. Two decisions stand between you and a functioning organization, along with quite a bit of work.

DECISION #1: FLAT OR DEEP

Another important dimension of organizational design is its depth. In case you aren't familiar with the trade-offs:

The more layers, the harder it is to know what's going on, because every layer filters the information those at the top receive. Even the best managers have to use their judgment as to what's important to pass on. The rest do everything they can to present the most optimistic picture possible, regardless of what's really going on.

Flatter organizations depend on strong managers who work together well, because strong managers who can collaborate effectively need leadership but not management. Leadership – pointing everyone in the right direction and making sure they buy into it – takes less time and attention than management, which includes all the effort and attention needed to keep track of what everyone is doing.

With more direct reports at every layer, the organization needs fewer layers.

Managers whose organizations have complex, judgment-based responsibilities ... practices (see sidebar) ... can handle fewer direct reports than those who have more easily measured, process-driven responsibilities. Those who manage practices spend more time with each person; the others are primarily responsible for process management where the whole point is to standardize the work at each step.

Put these principles together and you're in a position to decide whether to aggregate responsibilities under a middle manager or to handle them individually. To illustrate: In the organization we're using for the example we're following throughout this book, the CEO has decided to aggregate Human Resources, Purchasing, Facilities Management and a few other areas under a Chief Administrative Officer instead of having each report to him directly, creating a deeper organization in doing so.

DECISION #2: REALIGN, REORGANIZE, OR INTEGRATE

When you realign, workgroups remain intact but report up through a different management hierarchy. Reorganizations are more fundamental, eliminating many of the old workgroups and forming new ones.

As a general rule, only reorganize when you dramatically change how the work gets done. Otherwise, the workgroups you have are the workgroups you need.

Leave them alone.

Except: If the change is a merger or acquisition, everything becomes much, much messier. Unless the plan is to operate as a pure holding company that leaves the original businesses essentially intact, you're going to be taking some responsibilities (occasionally all responsibilities) that existed separately in the source companies and integrating them in the combined company.

Whether you realign, reorganize or integrate, managers who consider themselves to be losers with respect to the change will likely resist it, whether it's because the result shrinks the size of the organization they manage, the budget they command, or both. After you've finished redesigning the organizational chart, recognize which managers will figure they're on the losing end, plug this insight back into your stakeholder analysis, and figure out what you have to do to contain the damage.

Realignments

Realignments are less disruptive than reorganizations or integrations, but less doesn't mean trivial. Far from it. Because every realignment creates winners and losers among the managers (in the minds of employees if nowhere else), and because realignments result in employees reporting up through managers they don't know well instead of known quantities, realignments result in employees keeping their heads down and playing things safe until they've deciphered the new power structure.

Realign when you need to:

> Change the depth of the organization.
> Remove organizational barriers to process effectiveness ... and every time a process has to flow from one workgroup to another there's a barrier; when it has to flow between departments there's a bigger one.
> Disguise a management termination (but you won't fool anyone, so make sure you need to handle the situation this way).

For a realignment, whoever will lead the new organization should appoint the management team, announce the new organizational chart to employees, introduce the managers to them in case some employees don't happen to know their new manager ... and you're done.

Reorganizations and realignments are big deals to everyone involved. If they aren't, you're having too many of them.

Reorganizations

If you decide to reorganize, everything is (potentially) up for grabs because the roles that need to be filled in the new organization will be significantly different from the roles required in the old one.

If that isn't the case you should probably be realigning rather than reorganizing.

Which leaves you with yet another decision to make: How to decide which employees go where.

The most efficient approach is to appoint managers and employees to the new slots. It's quick, efficient, predictable, and less anxiety-producing than the other alternatives. Someone makes all the decisions and informs employees as part of the announcement.

The disadvantage should be obvious: By appointing managers and employees you make them powerless – the change happens to them rather than with them. Powerless is a synonym for victim, and victimized employees are more likely to resist the change.

That being the case you might decide to post the new positions instead and go through the lengthy process of allowing employees to apply for them. No alternative is as fair.

And no alternative is as bad an idea. Fair or not, the typical perception among everyone involved is, "Oh, boy! I get to apply for my own job!"

Beyond this disadvantage is the sheer time and effort involved. If even five managers and fifty individual contributors are directly affected by the change, you'll have to take the time to post, interview and select the five managers – figure a month – and then allow the additional time needed to post the non-managerial positions with the "new" managers interviewing the fifty applicants – another month.

And during those two months, a lot of the energy that should be devoted to getting work done will instead be absorbed by all the things uncertain and anxious employees do ... mostly grumbling and worrying.

The best approach we've come up with in our consulting is

somewhere between the two. It works like this:

1. ***Appoint the new managers.*** In most cases, whoever they're going to report to knows everyone who might be suitable personally through long association. Any interview process would be a sham, because any hiring manager who substitutes the quality of an interview for direct knowledge of the individual is a fool.

   Interviews are what you have to do because you don't know an individual personally – a poor second-best. Which might be what you have to do if you're centralizing a previously decentralized process, where you probably don't know all of the current managers well enough to make an informed decision.

   It's a tough situation because you probably do know one of them well enough, but excluding the others because you don't know them ... or because the executive in charge doesn't know them ... is a great way to generate tremendous distrust.

2. ***Announce the new organization.*** Let employees know what the new organizational chart will look like, who will be managing each of the boxes, and what the new roles will be.

3. ***Ask employees to list their preferences.*** Three is a good number. Let everyone know you'll try to accommodate as many as possible, but that your first responsibility is to make sure every role is filled by someone qualified to do the work. Also let them know that if they aren't assigned to one of their preferred roles, their new manager will be informed of their preference and will be responsible for helping them get there as part of the development plan that should be in place for every employee.

4. ***Get the managers together to horse-trade.*** For the new management team the available employees will mostly be known quantities. Handle the process more or less as football teams handle the annual draft – by each choosing their next-most-preferred employee in rotation. If you want to get fancy, change the order with each round.

5. ***Announce the results.***

Mergers and acquisitions

If you're going to run the combined entity as a holding company, leaving the original companies unchanged, you have no worries.

Also very little reason for the merger or acquisition, but that's
Someone Else's Problem. Otherwise ...

For the most part, handle mergers and acquisitions just as you'd
handle a reorganization. A few factors complicate them. Ignore
these factors and not only is the planned change dead on arrival, but
you'll get an entirely different change that can do as much damage
as a stink bomb in a perfume factory[33]. They are:

> *Different organizing strategies:* If the two original com-
panies are built around entirely different organizing principles, you'll have to rip at least one of them apart down to the
workgroup level, then combine equivalent workgroups.

> *Different cultures:* See Chapter 6 for guidance on this sub-
ject. Failing to manage the integration of differing corporate
cultures just about guarantees the failure of any merger or
acquisition.

> *Different processes and practices:* The two companies
will do the same work differently. The new company will either pick a winner or develop a new way of handling each
and every responsibility. In an acquisition the temptation will
be for the acquiring company to act as a conquering invader,
imposing its will on the conquered.

It's common. And it's stupid. If the acquired company
was worth buying, some of its processes and practices will
prove superior to those of the buyer.

So far as how to implement different processes and practices ... well, that's what this book is for.

> *Redundant managers:* A lot of them, and more as you look
higher in the organizational chart (with more employees
comes a need for more supervisors). Many will be excellent
at what they do and worth keeping, even though you have no
need for them in their old roles.

The best will command a great deal of loyalty from the
employees who report to them. Treat them badly and the
damage will range from demoralization to malicious obedience to an overt refusal to do more than the absolute minimum.

> *War games:* It's far from uncommon for executives and
managers from one, the other, or both companies involved
in a merger, and sometimes an acquisition, to plan strategies

---
33 A lot.

and tactics to gain control of the combined entity. Their focus will be power, not business benefit, and their actions will be covert. By the time you know it's happening, your plans will be in ruins.

And no, this isn't an overly dramatic account of things.

Whole books have been written about how to handle mergers and acquisitions. This brief account isn't intended to be a substitute, just a small set of signposts to get you pointed in the right direction.

Managing the transition

Transitions don't happen by themselves. Beyond the subjects that will be handled in later chapters ... training and communication in particular ... you have some planning to do.

Or, better, the new management team has some planning to do. The work got done the old way with employees in their old roles. If it's a realignment, the managers need to hand off their old responsibilities and assignments to each other. If it's a reorganization, every employee will have to hand off responsibilities and assignments.

Very important: If the change will be visible to customers, part of the relevant hand-offs is doing everything possible to make sure they see the benefit. And if the result of the realignment or reorganization will be to change who a customer works with, that change will take special care to prevent damage to the relationship.

That can be a lot of logistics to manage. There's no simple formula for figuring it all out, except that you shouldn't be the one to figure it all out.

You're the one who has to make sure everyone involved has taken the time to figure it out.

The Change (Centralized purchasing)

In our example, centralizing purchasing, a previously decentralized process, is a fundamental change in how the work will be done. It's a reorganization, or should be, because otherwise, here's what would happen:

> The same people would ...
> Do the same work ...
> Sitting in the same desks they sit in now ...
> With the same relationships, and therefore the same informal rules they've been operating under ...

> Which means they'll do the work the same old way …
> Undoubtedly with a dotted-line reporting relationship to whoever they currently have a solid-line reporting relationship to right now …
> With a solid-line reporting relationship added that lands in the CAO's office, far away and to total strangers who have other problems to deal with that are arguably more urgent and import …
> Resulting in no change other than a cosmetic one.

So it has to be a reorganization.

Because you're centralizing a previously decentralized process there's nothing for it but to have the CAO interview those currently responsible for managing it in each of the lines of business, choosing one to manage the responsibility at headquarters.

Depending how important the changed process is to the company and how easy or hard it is to bring a new employee up to full competence in it, either relocate those currently responsible to headquarters, or else encourage the Business Unit Heads to find other responsibilities for them and hire replacements at headquarters.

FACILITIES
They gotta have a place to sit.

Whether you're reorganizing or realigning, or even if you find you can leave the existing organizational chart entirely alone, the affected employees have to have a work environment that's conducive to the change you're responsible for making happen.

With reorganizations and realignments you first have to go through the nuts-and-bolts effort of finding enough room for everyone who has to work together, which sometimes creates a cascade of other remodeling and departmental moves, to make everything fit into the available space.

Unless you're very good at floor plans and office design, make friends with the Facilities Manager, who is.

Nothing particularly interesting here. The key is not to forget it, because you don't want to wake up at the end of the project, suddenly realizing the new organizations have no physical homes.

And you certainly don't want to leave it to the affected parties to figure out. The combination of altitude, position (corner, window or interior), size, enclosure (office or cubicle) and proximity to important people confers status, which makes this subject a potential political minefield[34].

The interesting part comes next. Business change almost always results in new process flows – changed ways of getting the work done – and also can lead to a change in the business culture (Chapter 6).

Sometimes, standard offices and cubicles will do the job. Among the annoyingly detailed but critically important questions to be answered:

> Who should sit where.
> The size of the cubicles and offices.
> The height of the cubicle walls.
> What equipment and tools employees will need – personal and shared.
> The "hours" rating of the chairs (did you know office chairs are rated by how many hours of continuous sitting they're good for?).
> How many conference rooms to include, how big each should be, and how they should be equipped[35].

And sometimes, standard offices and cubicles will be inconsistent with the process change, culture change or both.

Then there's the open floor plan, where workgroups share a "pod" with seating around the periphery and conference tables in the middle. If you need a lot of informal collaborations, pods are just the thing, even though everyone will wear out jokes about having become pod people early in the game.

Virtual offices

And then there's the increasingly popular option of switching to a virtual office.

This book would double in length if I tried to cover the subject of teleworkers in enough depth to be useful. If that's part of your plan, here's what you have to know right now:

> It's a complex subject with a lot of moving parts and alternatives. Don't "just do it" and expect a positive result.
> Managing teleworkers isn't just like managing local staff only you have to shout louder. Your training plan (Chapter 5) should include training for both managers and teleworkers on how to deal with their very different situation.

---

34 Other than "be very careful," I have no words of wisdom to offer in how to handle this challenge.
35 Whatever number you arrive at, add one. You'll need it.

> Provide "hoteling" cubicles for teleworkers when they do come in to the main office.
> Establish clear guidelines for who is *allowed* to telework, based on both roles and employee characteristics.
> Establish clear guidelines for which roles are *required* to telework and which are required to be on-site.
> Invest in remote collaboration technologies, and in the training that will make the difference between employees who can collaborate well using them and employees who become distracted by having to figure out how to operate the technology.
> Establish clear guidelines regarding the characteristics of home offices and for reimbursement for setting them up and equipping them with proper furniture, telephones and Internet connections.
> When forming teleworking teams, bring everyone together to get started face to face so the team has a change to gel. Remote collaboration works best after everyone has had a chance to get to know each other.
> Don't consider the General Counsel and Human Resources obstacles or check-boxes. Involve them heavily in the specifics. They'll keep you and the company out of trouble. And, they'll do a lot of the heavy lifting that otherwise would fall to you.

GOVERNANCE

Governance is the legal-sounding term for "how we make decisions."

Most companies have two governance processes at every level – the official one and the real one that precedes it.

The official one is described in terms of process steps, evaluation criteria, and approval levels. The unofficial one that precedes it is described, through folklore, in terms of who the decision-makers are, who tends to influence them, what their hot-buttons are, and how best to push them (or, less-wholesomely, in terms of tactical osculation).

Some business changes, especially those that are broad, deep, and strategic, will be at odds with the current approach to governance. For example, a company that says it's going to "push decision-making down to lower levels in order to make us more agile and effective" had better stop requiring CEO-level approval for $25,000 purchases, and if that proves impractical should certainly stop requiring five signatures before the CEO even sees the proposal.

Second example: A company that decides its future depends on customer loyalty will change its evaluation criteria to de-emphasize cost-cutting and risk-management in favor of prudent spending on customer care. It will, that is, or it will fail to make any meaningful improvements to customer loyalty.

Only the most profound changes will have a significant impact on governance at this level. Most changes will, however, profoundly affect governance inside whatever is being changed, even if the effect is unintended and accidental.

Take our example – centralizing Purchasing, a previously decentralized administrative process.

In a decentralized environment, you can bet many of those who need to buy something know how to schmooze to speed up the process. They know who has the authority to request a "confirming P.O." (where the purchaser provides a purchase order number to a merchant and gets the product immediately, and the paperwork catches up later) instead of requiring a signed, approved purchase requisition.

Centralize Purchasing and schmoozing won't work very well anymore. First of all, it's going to be through a telephone conversation rather than happening face to face. And second, it's going to be with a total stranger (initially at least) who will be less receptive to the pressure to just go along with it that's always the case when it comes from someone the decision-maker knows personally.

Even if a goal is to cut down on questionable purchases and exceptions in Accounts Payable, it's unlikely the company wants to become more overtly bureaucratic. Which means that as part of designing the change, the company should build in known ways to quickly and easily escalate exceptions when someone has a legitimate need to buy something quickly.

Somewhere in every business responsibility are decisions. Change how the business handles the responsibility and you'll probably need to change who makes the decisions, how they're made, or both. When you do, make sure the result is consistent with what you're trying to accomplish.

ACCOUNTING

When companies reorganize or realign responsibilities, they have to reallocate revenue and expense budgets. In theory this should be a straightforward analytical exercise. In practice it is easily politicized and more easily interpreted through a political lens.

Opinion: Do everything you can to keep all political considerations out of the accounting changes. Put a first-class financial analyst in charge of the exercise with instructions to consider only the intrinsic logic of the new organizational design.

If you want to get fancy about it and are operating in a poisonous political environment, have three financial analysts go through the exercise independently and average their results.

Many managers tie ownership of revenue and size of their expense budget to their sense of self-worth – it's personal.

Do what you can to de-personalize it, and to the extent you can't de-personalize it, plug the results into your stakeholder analysis, just as you did with the changes to the organizational chart.

COMPENSATION

Compensation is a complicated subject and you'll find plenty of books on the subject if your goal is to redesign the whole system.

Here you have two concerns: Whose compensation has to change, and how evaluation criteria need to change.

Neither is a particularly subtle point. What's peculiar is how often they're ignored.

Performer compensation changes

In business change of any size and significance, performers won't be doing the exact same work in the exact same way, because if they are, it isn't much of a change, is it? About the only exceptions are pure re-alignments – situations in which the root cause of the problem being addressed is that processes that could be entirely serviceable are breaking because they're crossing too many organizational boundaries.

Other than that, roles will change. Employees know, because we tell them every chance we get, that compensation is pegged to "the market," which means the company has compared what salary surveys reveal other companies are paying for employees to do similar kinds of work.

Change the work employees are doing and the skills they need to do it, and it's time for a fresh salary comparison.

Unless, that is, you want employees to conclude that the whole market-pay compensation system you've been explaining for so long is nothing but a sham.

Opinion: This isn't a matter of fairness. It isn't a matter of "doing the right thing." It's a matter of basic professionalism. You're changing the work, which means finding out what the market pays for the newly designed roles.

Here's the tough part: If the new roles pay more in the marketplace, the compensation change probably hasn't been built into the business case for the change.

And if the new roles pay less, you're stuck either letting employees know you'll be cutting their pay as part of the change ... an action unlikely to boost morale ... or overpaying compared to the marketplace.

What generally works best (which isn't necessarily as good as working well; this is the best of a bad lot of choices) is to inform the affected employees that their new roles are worth less in the marketplace, leave their compensation where it is, but freeze it until the marketplace catches up to them or they move on to higher-paying positions.

Evaluation criteria[36]

Given a choice between what managers and executives say is important and what they are paid to do, everyone in the company will do what they're paid to do.

Money talks, and it talks much louder than any other voice in the company.

Back in the early days of the quality movement, this knowledge was commonplace: If you say you want quality but pay bonuses on quantity, you'll get quantity every time.

At all levels affected by a change, base compensation and bonuses are based on a set of stated evaluation criteria. They might not fit the new situation. If they don't, make sure to change them so they do.

This insight isn't all that insightful. The hard part is measurement, covered in the last chapter.

The key, from the perspective of your structure plan, is to remember to do it.

Supervisory habits

Even if you take care of compensation issues and the formal evalu-

---

[36] When reviewing evaluation criteria, go back to Chapter 3 to review the process evaluation metrics. Even when compensation isn't directly affected, remember that metrics drive behavior.

ation criteria, it might not be enough. Everyone in a management or supervisory role is accustomed to overseeing the work according to a set of routines they've turned into habits. Change everything else and their habits are likely to remain ... for example, call center supervisors who are used to emphasizing abandon rates and talk times. Even when they know a new management goal is increased upselling, breaking the habit of encouraging the call center agents to speed things up isn't easy.

Your best tools in breaking these habits are awareness and management training. Don't skimp on either.

Executive compensation

While politically sensitive, executive compensation can be the single biggest barrier to successful business change. The point is obvious: Executives aren't going to support a change if their bonus depends on its failure.

The point is obvious. Doing something about the problem is what's difficult. Executive compensation formulas tend to be a bit complicated. Also, they generally are a product of the Board of Directors Compensation Committee, which means they are often political compromises, not engineered solutions.

If executive compensation is misaligned with your change, figure out the least disruptive solution, sell it to the CEO, nag him or her every so often, and hope for the best.

Table 7/ Business change checklist – Structure

Responsibility	Assignee	Completed
Determine[37] organizational strategy	CEO, Executive Team, Project Manager, Business Sponsor	
For shared services groups, determine service responsibilities and areas of authority	CEO, Shared Services Group Heads, Project Manager, Business Sponsor	
Determine the "unit of optimization" – generally either the enterprise or business unit levels	CEO, Project Manager, Business Sponsor	
Design/recommend organizational solution for affected areas of the business; identify solution as realignment, reorganization, or integration	Project Manager, Business Sponsor (Recommend), CEO (Approve)	
Select managers	Head of affected organizational area(s)	
Develop transition plan	Project Manager, Business Sponsor, affected executives and managers	
Design new facilities	Affected Operational Managers, Facilities Manager	
Document current official and unofficial governance processes associated with the business change	Project Manager, Project Team	
Design new governance processes, incorporating them into the new process design(s)	Project Manager, Project Team	
Determine necessary accounting and budgeting changes	Financial Analyst	
Modify executive, management, and staff compensation and performance evaluation criteria for consistency with the changed way of operating	Project Manager, Operational Managers, Human Resources	

---

37   "Determine" might be a matter of discovery, if the business change won't change this and will have to conform to it. Or, it might be a matter of design, if the business change is large enough in scope to call the current state into question.

CHAPTER 5/

TRAINING[38] PLAN

When the subject is business change and you promote the importance of training, nobody is likely to argue. The importance of training doesn't even qualify as an opinion or conclusion anymore.

It's assumed.

Assumptions being what they are, though, let's go through the logic anyway, just to make sure we're on solid ground.

You have at least three reasons to provide training to everyone affected by a business change. The first is to make sure they know how to fulfill their responsibilities under the new way of doing business. Fail to do this and (of course) the change will fail because your change will have turned competent employees into incompetent ones.

The second reason is related but more subtle: Employees, who know they are competent to fulfill their responsibilities the old way of doing things, will be justifiably anxious regarding their ability to fulfill their responsibilities the new way of doing things.

This lack of confidence, left unaddressed, results in an entirely predictable resistance to the change.

Then there's the third reason: Shared expectations. It isn't enough for everyone to understand their own roles. They need to have confidence everyone understands their roles, the hand-offs among them, and how it all will come together to work better than

---

38 There's a useful distinction to be made between training and education. Training is about skills. Education is about knowledge and understanding. This chapter is about both, and won't worry about the distinction – "training" will be used to cover both topics.

the way things work now.

You need employees who are both competent and confident.

Confidence and competence aren't limited to performers, either. Every stakeholder needs to be confident the new way of doing things will work and that they'll have no trouble working with it.

And ... even employees who favor what you're doing might find themselves dealing with some of the emotional detritus that accompanies the transition from the old to the new. Give them some tools for coping and they'll be less likely to be caught off guard.

FORMAL TRAINING

You're changing some employees' jobs. They need to know how to succeed in their new roles. So tell them.

A few tips:

Engage the professionals early

Somewhere in your company – probably but not necessarily Human Resources – is a department whose responsibility is making sure employees have the training necessary to do their jobs well. Bring them into the change initiative early, so they're part of the design discussions. You want them to have the full context. They'll want to have the full context too.

Don't let the training professionals sell employees short

Every so often you'll run into training professionals who have developed the peculiar notion that most employees aren't very capable. Very likely it's because they're gauged on how well employees retain what they teach, leading them to teach only what's most easily retained[39].

Whatever the reason, if you find yourself working with this breed of trainer, don't let them persuade you to dumb down the employee positions into responsibilities any monkey could fulfill. Their job is to help employees succeed at the roles you design, not to design roles so they're excessively easy to succeed in.

Show employees how to do their jobs, not how to use the tools

More precisely, show them how to do their jobs the new way, using

---

39 Yet another example of getting what you measure, whether or not it's the result you actually want. See Chapter 3.

the new tools: "Here's how you create a new purchase requisition. Here's how you select an existing vendor. Here's how you submit a request to add a vendor, and how to continue creating the requisition, and how to save it as a draft until the new vendor has been added to the system." And so on.

Often, it isn't done that way. Here's why:

Because most business change projects involve the use of new software tools, there's a mistaken notion in some circles that these are "IT projects." That being the case, a great deal of the training developed for these projects shows employees how to operate the software: "When you click here, this happens. When you click there, this other thing happens."

The results are as predictable as they are avoidable: When the time comes to get to work, employees figure out how to use the software to do their jobs, and each one figures it out just a bit differently from everyone else.

And so, one employee puts terms and conditions in the P.O. Comments field, a second puts them in the Extended Description field of the last item on the purchase order, and a third enters them in the Vendor Alternate Name field. This messes up the process whenever a work item flows from an employee who has decided to improvise one way to a second employee who prefers to improvise a different way. At a minimum, the second employee will spend time and effort adjusting the improvisations.

Another, longer-term consequence is that this situation will mess up the database something fierce, ensuring: (1) The chartering of a data clean-up project three years after the initial software deployment; and (2) endless sneering about dumb end-users by members of the software development team.

Provide context, not just job-specific skills

Employees need to know how to succeed in their new roles. They also need to understand how their roles fit into the bigger picture. Sometimes, they need to know to make intelligent decisions about a specific, unusual situation. Sometimes it's so they know who to talk to when something seems out of line.

And sometimes it's to make sure they don't waste their time handling an "exception" whose handling is built into the system ... for example, a purchase requisition that's on hold waiting for a vendor to be added, where in our mythical example the system's designers were thoughtful enough to have it automatically release requisitions once the vendor has been added, without any additional employee intervention.

Brand training[40]

Many business changes are visible to outside paying customers. By definition, these changes will have an impact on the company brand, defined as the expectation customers have about what doing business with your company will be like.

Make sure customer-facing employees – that's anyone whose work might be visible to outside, paying customers – receive training in how to "be the brand" so that the impact of the change on the brand is positive, consistent, and intentional.

Train just in time

Just in case you didn't already know this, new knowledge and skills have a short half-life. Hold training sessions no more than two weeks before the go-live date.

Don't worry – if you've engaged the professionals, they'll insist on this.

Tailor training to the level of aptitude and confidence

Some employees are comfortable with computers, learn quickly, and only need "delta training" – a comparison of how things used to be with how they are now.

Other employees are still intimidated by all things digital, are slower on the uptake, and lack confidence besides.

Rather than providing one-size-fits-all training, ask managers who will need what level of training and slot employees into sessions adapted to their abilities.

Certify knowledge and skills

Build exercises and tests into the training flow, both to make sure employees learned the material and to help them retain it.
Don't worry about this either. The professionals will build it in as a matter of course.

Provide floorwalkers or triage centers

For the first week after you go live, make sure there are experts

---

40 Credit where it's due: My friend and client Daniel Gumnit called this issue to my attention a long time ago.

in the new way of doing things, close at hand, ready to answer all questions. Ideally, you'll be able to have them physically present where the work takes place, so they can provide immediate assistance, before an employee decides to improvise.

Two approaches to doing so: Either organize them as floorwalkers, in a position to spot a raised hand and walk over, or commandeer close-by conference rooms for use as triage centers, where employees who experience problems can go to get them resolved.

Failing on-site support make sure employees know they have access to a well-staffed hotline – one that never leads to them hearing the phrase, "Your call is important to us …"

One more tip: Engage the entire project team in providing this support. They are, after all, the experts. Beyond that they'll find the exercise gratifying as they see the results of all their hard work in productive use.

Don't assume you did it right

After the first day, and again at the end of the first week, poll the affected employees. Find out where they're confident, where the training fell short, and what they've figured out and think should be shared with their co-workers (this last will include a lot of the improvising you wanted to prevent, so expect it and figure out how to gently steer everyone back on track).

Wherever the training fell short, make sure to follow up with an additional session.

TRANSITION TRAINING

As mentioned last chapter, moving from the way things were to the way things will be takes more than explaining how things are now supposed to work and counting on everyone involved to figure out how to get from here to there.

You'll need a transition plan. Then, in addition to educating everyone in the new way of doing things, you'll have to provide the roadmap for getting from here to there and help everyone understand the part they'll have to play in making the transition happen smoothly.

One tip: Beyond the steps themselves, make sure everyone involved in the transition expects the road to be bumpy. If they're expecting rocks and potholes, every bit of smoothness will be a pleasant surprise. If they're expecting new asphalt, every bump will be evidence the new way of doing things won't work.

COPING SKILLS TRAINING

There's another dimension to training – helping managers help their employees, and especially accepters, understand the emotional dislocations that often accompany a transition from one situation to a different situation.

The short version: In a small way, many employees will be going through a grieving process – the sense of loss that accompanies giving up the familiar and moving to a new situation that is unfamiliar.

Even changes that appear to be relatively minor can lead to disproportionate responses, as employees discover the unwritten rules are now different, and what used to work no longer does.

Without preparation, they'll experience the standard five stages of grief: Denial, anger, anger, anger, and more anger. They won't even know why.

And if the change is more significant, leading to layoffs, changes in reporting relationships, and the loss of importance of hard-won skills, the grieving will be very real.

Make sure employees know to expect this. And make sure to give their managers a toolkit for dealing with employees who get stuck in the anger stage and can't bring themselves to move on.

That's the short version. For the long version, I can't do better than to refer you to William Bridges' classic work on the subject, *Managing Transitions: Making the Most of Change* (1991).

STAKEHOLDER TRAINING

Whatever the change is that you're putting into place, it's unlikely that it will only be visible to performers. Probably, the change will affect customers[41], other employees, vendors, or some combination of the three.

If there's any change in how external stakeholders will have to interact with the new way of doing things, make sure they know what they have to do.

Also make sure they know why you're making the change, and do what you can to persuade them it's an improvement over the old system ... but that's a subject best held for Chapter 7 – the Communications Plan.

---

41 No, no, no. I'm talking about Real, Paying Customers. There's no such thing as an "internal customer." I thought we already had this discussion. In case we didn't, read chapter 9 of *Keep the Joint Running: A Manifesto for 21st Century Information Technology* (Bob Lewis, 2008).

Last word about stakeholders: Especially when the change involves a process with a lot of informal workarounds and folklore, stakeholders who know how to work the system and work around the system are also likely to get stuck in the anger stage of the grieving process.

It will help if whoever designed the new way of doing things took the time to learn the folklore and informal workarounds and built them into their design.

Otherwise, the stakeholders will have every right to be annoyed.

THE CHANGE (CENTRALIZED PURCHASING)

Continuing to use centralization of non-strategic sourcing as our example, here's the skeleton training plan:

> *Formal skills training:* Because the company in question was run more like a holding company than as an integrated service provider, each line of business used its own software to manage its purchasing process. The consolidated process will make use of the parent company's systems.

  All employees in the newly formed centralized purchasing department will be trained in the use of this system to review and approve purchase requisitions, create and transmit purchase orders, notify Accounts Payable on receipt of invoice, and so forth.

  (No training will be needed in Accounts Payable. Its job has been simplified, as it now will only have to handle purchase orders generated by a single system instead of by several different ones.)

> *Context training:* Very little will be needed for this change. Purchasing employees will be coached in how to support process stakeholders and deal with their initial frustrations … in particular, everyone who needs to buy something and is used to knowing the ins and outs of their line-of-business purchasing process.

> *Tailoring to level of aptitude:* Not necessary – every member of the new Purchasing Department is already familiar with purchasing concepts, and with using automated tools to make everything happen.

> *Floorwalkers/Triage Center:* Both will be provided during the first week of operation. Two members of the project team will be available at any given moment, on a rotating sched-

ule. One will walk the floor to handle immediate questions, the other will be in the Triage Center (a small nearby conference room) to track down any system glitches that turn up and need to be addressed.

> **Transition training:** The project team has decided to centralize staff under its new management all at once, but to stage the process transition one line of business at a time. This means the need for transition training will be minimal – there won't be any periods of time when specific employees have to handle some purchase orders the old way and some the new way.

> **Coping skills training:** Provided to the Purchasing Manager, as she will be managing the employees most likely to need help. In addition, for those employees who have been relocated to headquarters, Human Resources will provide an "introduction to the area" session, to acquaint them with what their new home city has to offer.

> **Stakeholder training:** The team's trainer, working with Purchasing, developed a one-page purchasing guide, available on the company intranet. In addition, the trainer polled the purchasing staff from each line of business to find out which employees in their area are the heaviest purchasing users, and will provide them with a one-hour in-person orientation to the new process.

Table 8 / Business change checklist – Training

Responsibility	Assignee	Completed
Training professional(s) assigned to project	Project Manager	
Training focus: How to perform new roles, using the new tools	Trainers	
Training includes context, not just skills	Trainers	
Floorwalkers assigned	Project Manager	
Transition training developed	Project Manager	
Coping skills training developed	Human Resources	
Stakeholder training program developed	Depends on Stakeholder	
Training scheduled (1 – 2 weeks prior to deployment)	Project Manager	

CHAPTER 6/

CULTURE CHANGE PLAN

"Culture" is one of those words. It's like the spleen. Most people are pretty sure they have one. They just aren't exactly clear about what it is or does.

We'll start with a definition borrowed from the field of Cultural Anthropology: Culture is the learned behavior people exhibit in response to their environment.

It's a good definition for scientific investigation. Behavior is observable, where the other stuff of culture – rules, knowledge, attitudes and such – must be inferred. It's restricted in scope just enough to be useful as well: It deals only with behaviors that are in response to an individual's environment, not all behaviors of any kind.

It isn't, however, a perfect definition. Even though attitudes aren't directly observable, they play the same role in culture that DLLs play in Microsoft Windows: You might not know much about what's inside them, but you know they're what make things work ... and, at times, fail to work.

Sort of like the spleen, come to think of it.

We'll stick with the Cultural Anthropologists' definition, not because we're taking the scientific view that anything you can't observe isn't worth worrying about, but because attempts to change attitudes generally turn into the sort of preachy lectures usually reserved for parents who enjoy watching their teen-aged offspring's eyes roll.

But we're getting ahead of ourselves. Before we talk about

changing culture, we need to talk about how to describe it.

CHARACTERIZING CULTURE

The first step in planning a culture change is characterizing the culture – describing it in an organized way. After you describe it, you might decide it's just fine the way it is, but you won't be in a position to make that decision until you have a clear picture of what you're dealing with.

The definition itself guides the process. Culture is how employees respond to their environment, which means every organization has a culture. With few exceptions, generally the result of unintegrated mergers and acquisitions, organizations have a culture and many sub-cultures. One way or another, as is also true of strategies, missions and values, there is a culture. It's there for you to discover and describe, not to define from scratch.

Culture being defined in terms of how employees respond to their environment, to characterize culture, start with different sorts of situations and describe how employees respond to them. For example:

> > *In a crisis* we all pull together and don't worry about who's supposed to have which roles and responsibilities.
> > *When under time pressure,* everyone does whatever they feel like without consulting the experts who are responsible for a function.
> > *When someone from outside our organization complains about us* to employees who work here, our employees express no loyalty. Instead, they add to the complaints.
> > *When someone in the business raises an issue about IT's performance* we do a very good of listening to them, conveying our concern, and avoiding sounding defensive about it.
> > Everyone really cares about *the problems we face*.
> > I hear a lot of complaining *about problems*, but not much in the way of solutions.
> > As far as *taking care of the basics* is concerned, we're good at figuring things out. We don't get hung up with unnecessary formalities – our employees focus on getting the job done.
> > We're completely disorganized. No matter *what the situation calls for,* every employee does things differently

based only on their personal preferences, and the result is we're constantly reinventing the wheel.

> We say we reach a consensus *in a meeting*, but after the meeting people do whatever they did before if they don't like the decision.

> We're very good at involving everyone *when making decisions* so that everyone has buy-in.

> *In most situations,* our employees help each other out, giving each other informal on-the-job training whenever necessary.

> *No matter what the situation*, we never document anything – everything happens by folklore, and if a key employee calls in rich[42], there's a good chance nobody will know how to take care of their responsibilities.

> Our employees show a lot of *loyalty* to the business leader in charge of their area.

> We're heavily siloed – employees in one part of the company don't *trust* anyone in any other part of the company.

These are just some examples of what you might uncover in determining the current state of the culture.

Take a second look at the above list and you'll notice that it includes only seven characteristics, not fourteen. The statements are in pairs, and the only difference between the statements in each pair is whether the recorder happens to like or dislike the behavior in question.

This matters. Practice the art of describing every cultural trait in both positive and negative terms, because with very few exceptions, cultural responses are neither good nor bad in any absolute sense. Mostly, they're good fits for some circumstances; bad fits for other circumstances.

As evidence, examine your reaction to, "We're hopelessly bureaucratic and rigidly regimented. Every member of the organization receives instructions so tightly described that there's no room for creativity or individual expression, and everyone here likes it that way."

Pretty bad, isn't it? You certainly wouldn't want to run, for example, an ad agency that way.

If, on the other hand, you're responsible for the marching band

---

42 And thanks to the IT team at Seattle Central Community College for providing this excellent alterative to the usual "is hit by a bus."

that's putting on a halftime show that will be broadcast nationwide, it's exactly what you need.

As leader of the band, because it's exactly what you need, you'd describe the same culture quite differently. Give it a try and see what you come up with.

So to characterize your current culture, assemble the change

Table 9/ **Culture change worksheet, step 1:** *Characterizing the culture*

Situation	Current Response (Positive)	Current Response (Negative)
Crisis	We all pull together and don't worry about who's supposed to have which roles and responsibilities.	Everyone does whatever they feel like without consulting the experts who are responsible for a function.
Externally identified performance issue	When someone in the business raises an issue about IT's performance we do a very good of listening to them, conveying our concern, and avoiding sounding defensive about it.	Our employees feel no loyalty towards IT. They love to join in the criticism.
Internally identified performance issues	Everyone really cares about what we should do better.	A lot of complaining, but not much in the way of solutions.
Day-to-day work	We're good at figuring things out. We don't get hung up with unnecessary formalities – our employees focus on getting the job done.	We're completely disorganized. Every employee does things differently based only on their personal preferences, and the result is we're constantly reinventing the wheel.
Work style	Our employees help each other out, giving each other informal on-the-job training whenever necessary.	We never document anything – everything happens by folklore, and if a key employee "calls in rich," there's a good chance nobody will know how to take care of their responsibilities.
Problem analysis	We have a strong focus on accountability.	Our first response to any problem is to assign blame.
Loyalty	Our employees show a lot of loyalty to the business leader in charge of their area.	We're heavily siloed – employees in one part of the company don't trust anyone in any other part of the company.

ringleaders (the business sponsor, champion or champions if you think they'll have helpful insights, and whichever key stakeholders you consider to be part of your trusted inner circle).

Acquaint them with the situation/response way of describing culture, and have at it. Then, as you and the rest of the leadership team review your culture, pay attention to how each individual phrases his or her likes and dislikes – it's illuminating. Challenge the participants to rephrase every trait so you have both a positive and negative version of each.

Organize the results so that for every situation, everyone sees both the positive and negative description (Table 9).

These statements aren't particularly brief. That's deliberate. This is just your loyal author's opinion: Vision and mission statements should be brief, simple, and catchy. Descriptions of culture should be thoughtful and thorough. That takes more than a five word sentence.

DESIGNING THE CHANGE

Having described the current culture, you're in a position to decide what about it might be in conflict with your planned change.

There's no magic process here. No step-by-step analysis. Walk through your culture change worksheet one row at a time with your inner circle and ask whether anyone thinks that row is a likely obstacle, and why.

The Change (Centralized purchasing)

We've been using the centralization of a previously decentralized administrative process, namely purchasing, as an example. Look through the list and it's pretty clear that the cultural elements most likely to get in the way of this change are those associated with day-to-day work, work style, and loyalty.

Day-to-day work and work style will be barriers because one of the goals of the new process is to handle a particular responsibility in a more organized, standardized way that makes sure everything is properly documented.

Loyalty will be a barrier for all the obvious reasons: For employees in each of the lines of business to make use of a centralized administrative process they'll have to have some trust that employees at corporate headquarters will take care of them properly. And that's the opposite of a siloed attitude about the organization.

Update the culture change table (Table 10) to reflect these insights: Use the "Matters" column to check off which cultural traits have to change (they matter). Use the "Desired Response" column to describe how they have to change.

CHANGING THE CULTURE

Now that we know what about the culture has to change, and how, we're ready for the tough challenge: How to go about it.

Table 10/ **Culture change worksheet, step 2:** *Designating which cultural traits matter for a particular change, and how they have to change*

Situation	Current response (Positive)	Current response (Negative)	Matters	Desired response
Crisis	We all pull together and don't worry about who's supposed to have which roles and responsibilities.	Everyone does whatever they feel like without consulting the experts who are responsible for a function.		
Externally identified performance issue	When someone in the business raises an issue about IT's performance we do a very good of listening to them, conveying our concern, and avoiding sounding defensive about it.	Our employees feel no loyalty towards IT. They love to join in the criticism.		
Internally identified performance issues	Everyone really cares about what we should do better.	A lot of complaining, but not much in the way of solutions.		
Day-to-day work	We're good at figuring things out. We don't get hung up with unnecessary formalities – our employees focus on getting the job done.	We're completely disorganized. Every employee does things differently based only on their personal preferences, and the result is we're constantly reinventing the wheel.	X	We handle routine tasks in a well-defined and organized way so we can become as efficient as possible.
Work style	Our employees help each other out, giving each other informal on-the-job training whenever necessary.	We never document anything – everything happens by folklore, and if a key employee "calls in rich," there's a good chance nobody will know how to take care of their responsibilities.	X	Our employees help each other out. While they provide on-the-job training where appropriate, they also point colleagues to written policies and procedures when they exist.
Problem analysis	We have a strong focus on accountability.	Our first response to any problem is to assign blame.		
Loyalty	Our employees show a lot of loyalty to the business leader in charge of their area.	We're heavily siloed – employees in one part of the company don't trust anyone in any other part of the company.	X	Our employees help each other out, wherever they sit in the organizational chart.

Back to the definition again: Culture is the learned behavior employees exhibit *in response to their environment.*

You aren't going to change learned behavioral responses overnight. With most employees you probably won't ever be able

to change them. Much of the learning that led to their responses preceded their employment in your company. When it comes
right down to it, a lot of the most important learning preceded
their adulthood.

What you can change
is the environment em-
ployees experience and
respond to. Change the
environment and you
change the culture.

Easier said than done,
because most of the en-
vironment employees are
responding to is the be-
havior of other employ-
ees, which means culture
is the behavior employ-
ees exhibit in response to
the behavior employees
exhibit in response to the
behavior employees ex-
hibit ... on and on, *ad in-
finitum* (Figure 6).

Culture appears to
be a Gordian Knot, with
no obvious loose ends to
grab hold of. Everyone's
expectations of everyone
else conspire to keep it
as it is. It's a case of infinite regression, intracta-

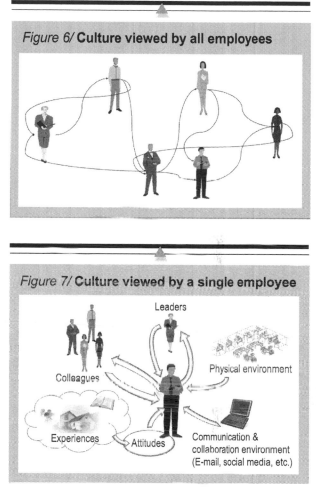

Figure 6/ **Culture viewed by all employees**

Figure 7/ **Culture viewed by a single employee**

ble and unsolvable, impossible to untie. Viewed this way you might
decide to take Alexander's approach, cutting the knot by cutting all
of the offending employees.

It seems to make sense: As you can't change how employees respond to their environment – unless you change out all of your employees – and can't change a lot of their environment either ... also
unless you change out a lot of your employees ... to change the culture you'll have to replace your employees.

But the situation isn't as hopeless as all that, nor would replacing your employees accomplish very much, because far from being a case of infinite regression, the regression involved in culture change is seriously finite.

Figure 7 tells the story. Culture is the learned behavior employees exhibit in response to their environment. Their environment is multifaceted.

A lot of it is beyond your influence ... their colleagues' behavior, as already mentioned; also all of their past and present outside experiences and the attitudes these have encouraged and continue to encourage.

You can, however, change their physical environment, communications and collaboration tools, and the leadership behavior that has more impact on the corporate culture than all other influences combined.

Physical environment

We touched on this in Chapter 4 from the perspective of the influence facilities can have on process effectiveness. The impact on culture can be, if anything, even more profound.

Microsoft famously gives everyone an office. That encourages heads-down concentration but almost has to discourage informal collaboration.

Intel was at one time noted for having no offices at all. Even the top executives worked in open cubicles. Intel also provided large numbers of small, conveniently located conference rooms that provided privacy and acoustical isolation, to encourage employees to work together whenever they needed to, but not by default.

Low cubicle walls will encourage informal discussions. High ones, which force employees to walk around them, will discourage it.

An open floor plan ("pods") draw teams into informal conversations. They encourage collaboration but make heads-down work more difficult.

Virtual teams ... teams whose members are scattered all over the landscape, communicating solely via electronic channels ... are less likely to form close friendships and more likely to treat each other as "black box" work generators. They facilitate heads-down concentration even more than private offices.

And so on. Form follows function, so start with the culture you want to encourage and design a physical environment that encourages it.

Communications environment

In the 1990s, when e-mail finally became pervasive in corporate America, it drove an unplanned and very significant change in most corporate cultures. Two, really, maybe more.

One change was a significant increase in informality, probably because e-mail made it easy for anyone to send anyone else a quick note. That drove a lot more communication around the chain of command.

The other change was a shift in how executives and managers thought about the task of communicating, changing their emphasis from careful phrasing and importance-conveying look-and-feel, to quick turnaround and never mind the frills.

What drove this shift was that e-mail meant they were typing their memos themselves, rather than dictating them to their secretaries. Those who resisted this change generally found themselves under pressure from their peers, because their old habits let to their acquiring reputations for responding too slowly.

In the early 2000s quite a few companies tried to institute Knowledge Management Systems – an attempt at deliberate culture change built around a new collaboration technology. Knowledge management has not, at this juncture, become pervasive.

Meanwhile, back on the Internet, MySpace and Facebook pioneered the notion of social media and experienced colossal growth (although News Corp has done a terrific job of destroying MySpace). Social media have been immensely successful as vehicles for knowledge sharing, although at times not the sort of knowledge sharing parents might be comfortable with.

At knowledge sharing, Facebook's success pales in comparison to Wikipedia, without question the most successful knowledge management system of all time.

Our take-home lessons from this brief history? One is that communication and collaboration environments have to be engaging to be successful. Another is that changing the culture by providing new communications tools is a crap shoot – it might take hold, it might not, and the change you get might not be the change you expected.

The third lesson: Tool-enabled culture change doesn't succeed because you add something to the job description (the probable flaw in trying to make Knowledge Management Systems successful). To the extent you can plan it at all, figure employees will adopt these tools to the extent their operation is easily understood, company management exerts only limited control, and employees perceive personal benefit in their use – and whether the benefit is ego gratification, social engagement, or just that the tools are fun to use doesn't much matter.

BAD FITS

Some employees don't fit the corporate culture. That was probably true before the change you're leading. It will be true after you've succeeded in implementing the change.

Depending on how you're trying to change the culture, they might or might not be the same employees: If you're trying to loosen up an organization that's too bureaucratic, employees who were misfit renegades might now find themselves in the mainstream while large numbers of heads-down by-the-book employees are bewildered and overcome by the chaos.

When you interview job applicants, something you look for is good cultural fit. When changing the culture, be even more alert.

The situation is no different from any other aspect of a change. With culture as with every other dimension of the change, you'll find supporters, resisters, and adapters. The guidelines from chapter 1 apply here just as much as they apply to any new process you're putting into place.

The only difference is that it's easy to spot an employee who refuses to follow a process. Refusing to follow a culture is a bigger leadership challenge. Ultimately, it will be up to each employee's reporting manager to deal with employees who no longer fit the culture.

It's up to you to alert affected reporting managers to the challenge.

Leadership

This is the big one.

Changing the physical environment and enhancing tools for communication and collaboration are good ideas. But in the end, the most important aspect of the environment employees respond to is the behavior of the company's leaders.

Which means the most important tool at your disposal for changing the culture is changing leader behavior. Culture starts at the top and works its way down.

The analytical technique for demonstrating how leader behavior connects to culture is labor-intensive, time-consuming, and probably not all that useful to you: It involves interviewing large numbers of employees to get an accurate picture of how they think they respond to different situations, and how they think the company leadership would react were they to respond differently.

The alternative is to use your knowledge of what makes people tick, and your own knowledge of how the company's executives and managers tend to react to different sorts of employee behavior to figure out the connection. It usually isn't all that complicated a question:

> If the culture needs to become more informal, with a lot more peer-to-peer connections, leaders

probably enforce working through the chain of command and express displeasure whenever anything happens they haven't pre-approved. If they want the culture to change, they need to start asking, "Why are you asking my permission? Work with whoever you need to work with. Tell me when it's ready for me to look at, and let me know if you need my help."

> If employees don't sweat the details and figure sloppy work is just fine, there's a strong chance business leaders consider the "view from 10,000 feet" to be fine-grained understanding. If that needs to change, they need to start asking, "Walk me through this so I understand the specifics. The devil is in the details, and I want to make sure we've covered all the bases."

> If everyone's first response to a problem is to keep their heads down until it blows over, while doing their best to make sure the problem itself stays hidden from management as long as possible ... it's a near certainty business leaders' first reaction to any problem is to assign blame.

That won't be how they describe their behavior, of course, but that doesn't matter. What matters is that problems result in punishments – the leader behavior that usually underlies a culture of blame.

The challenge isn't figuring out the connection between the culture and leader behavior. It's that as a change leader, the need to change the culture can and usually will put you in an awkward situation: You know the culture. You recognize how it reinforces the status quo and will actively discourage the change you're responsible for making happen. And, you have a pretty good idea of what the company's leaders will have to do differently.

One of *Aesop's Fables* covers this territory nicely – the one about belling the cat.

In case you somehow missed this one: A bunch of mice figure out they'd be less likely to become dinner if the cat wore a bell, alerting them to its approach. They all agreed this was a terrific idea. Then one of the mice asked who was going to volunteer to put the bell on the cat.

There are only two possible volunteers for this particular cat belling: You and the business sponsor. And it's entirely possible the business sponsor will turn out to be one of the cats[43].

---

43 Especially if Stan Katz is the sponsor. But I digress, and just insulted every reader named Stan Katz. Sorry, Stan.

There's no easy solution. But then, you knew when you took on the "driver" role that you were going to have to stick your neck out from time to time. So here's how you go about it:

> *Assess the importance:* Decide whether the culture changes you've identified, and the modifications to leadership behavior needed to cultivate the culture change, are crucial, significant, nice to have, or trivial in their impact. If they aren't significant (at least) you can stop. You have more important issues requiring your attention.

> *Figure the odds:* Think about who you're dealing with – the CEO, CFO, COO and so on. How likely is it that they'll take any of this seriously enough to make the required changes? If you can't honestly give it at least a 50/50 then don't take it on at all.

> *Reinforce the behavior:* Just because the leaders agree, it doesn't mean they'll appreciate you or anyone else pointing out when they backslide. It might sound hokey; it's still a good idea to agree to a code phrase that constitutes a "safe mode" for pointing out backsliding.

> *Figure the timing:* Culture change is a slow process. Often, six months isn't unreasonable for seeing the first glimmerings that something is different and two years isn't too early a time to determine whether or not the change has been successful. Use your judgment regarding the likely time frame, and when in doubt, a pessimistic estimate is more likely to be accurate than an optimistic one.

If the time you think will be required for culture change to be noticeable will be too late to do any good ... if your change will have succeeded or failed long before the change in culture has had a chance to take hold ... then don't pin your hopes on the change in culture.

Instead, figure out how to make the change happen without it.

Whatever you decide, keep the business sponsor in the loop as a full co-conspirator. Talk over the nature of the culture changes you think would be desirable, how leader behavior ... including his/her behavior ... would need to change to achieve it, and whether you think it's feasible or not.

And, if the two of you conclude it is, agree on which of you will be the cat-beller.

THE CHANGE (CENTRALIZED PURCHASING)

Here's an example – how to change the culture in an intentional way so it's a better fit for the centralized purchasing function we're trying to institute in our mythical enterprise:

Physical environment

We're centralizing non-strategic sourcing, forming a small new team to handle it. It isn't an assembly-line style process either. It's more of a practice, where each team member handles all of the work for a single request, front to back.

Our culture change worksheet (Table10) tells us we want employees to follow a known, documented process; also that we want them to help each other out. That means you need a lot of cross-training and informality, so everyone knows what anyone knows.

On the other hand, purchasing includes a lot of telephone work, and a completely open environment would result in employees irritating each other rather than trusting each other.

So we settle on cubicles with low walls.

And purchasing employees deal with vendors a lot, so we also provide a few conference rooms for when the vendors show up on site.

Communications environment

No process design is ever complete, and that includes the newly centralized purchasing process that constitutes our example.

The performers are the ones who have to figure out workarounds for whatever the process designers miss.

Preventing this would be crippling, but allowing every employee to develop different workarounds leads to problems, as already mentioned, and would violate our goals for day-to-day work and work style.

To address this, we decide to implement a wiki for the performers to use as an easy way to document newly-discovered workarounds. Two wrinkles: We include an editorial workflow component, so the process manager must review the workarounds and can, if necessary, intervene. And, to encourage employees to make use of the wiki, all entries can be signed so employees can get some public recognition for their work if they want it.

That covers day-to-day work and work style. How about the loyalty culture?

We need to do everything possible to build trust in the process,

Table 11/ Culture change worksheet, step 3: How to encourage the change

Situation	Current response (Positive)	Current response (Negative)	Matters	Desired response	How to achieve it
Crisis	We all pull together and don't worry about who's supposed to have which roles and responsibilities.	Everyone does whatever they feel like without consulting the experts who are responsible for a function.			
Externally identified performance issue	When someone in the business raises an issue about IT's performance we do a very good of listening to them, conveying our concern, and avoiding sounding defensive about it.	Our employees feel no loyalty towards IT. They love to join in the criticism.			
Internally identified performance issues	Everyone really cares about what we should do better.	A lot of complaining, but not much in the way of solutions.			
Day-to-day work	We're good at figuring things out. We don't get hung up with unnecessary formalities – our employees focus on getting the job done.	We're completely disorganized. Every employee does things differently based only on their personal preferences, and the result is we're constantly reinventing the wheel.	X	We handle routine tasks in a well-defined and organized way so we can become as efficient as possible.	> **Physical environment:** Low-walled cubicles. > **Communication tools:** A wiki, so employees can easily document new techniques. > **Leader behavior:** Don't bypassing the process, help others work it, inform the process manager of problems.
Work style	Our employees help each other out, giving each other informal on-the-job training whenever necessary.	We never document anything – everything happens by folklore, and if a key employee "calls in rich," there's a good chance nobody will know how to take care of their responsibilities.	X	Our employees help each other out. While they provide on-the-job training where appropriate, they also point colleagues to written policies and procedures when they exist.	> **Physical environment:** Low-walled cubicles. > **Communication tools:** A wiki, so employees can easily document new techniques. > **Leader behavior:** Don't bypassing the process, help others work it, inform the process manager of problems.

Table 11/ Culture change worksheet, step 3 - Continued

Situation	Current response (Positive)	Current response (Negative)	Matters	Desired response	How to achieve it
Problem analysis	We have a strong focus on accountability.	Our first response to any problem is to assign blame.			
Loyalty	Our employees show a lot of loyalty to the business leader in charge of their area.	We're heavily siloed – employees in one part of the company don't trust anyone in any other part of the company.	X	Our employees help each other out, wherever they sit in the organizational chart.	> Physical environment: No impact. > Communication tools: Instant messaging - another informal stakeholder communication channel. > Leader behavior: Nothing that's achievable.

and that means building trust between those who will make use of the process and the performers who make it happen. And trust is difficult in the face of geographic separation (which might mean different countries, states, zip codes, floors, or even just being on opposite sides of a hallway).

We can't solve this challenge entirely, but we can reduce its impact. One step we're taking is to add instant messaging to the communications mix, to encourage informal communication between process stakeholders and process performers.

Leadership

For centralized purchasing, when it comes to day-to-day work and work style, the most important change in leader behavior will be radical for the executives who run our mythical company: They'll have to ostentatiously follow the process every time they need to buy something, instead of being the ones who use their authority to bypass it.

Even more important, they'll need to change the role they habitually play when someone else asks for their help because the process is getting in their way: They need to help that person work the process rather than helping them bypass it.

And, if it turns out the process doesn't handle some situations as well as it should, they need to let the process manager know about the problem and the importance of fixing it.

These two changes, you figure, are important enough, likely enough, and can have a fast enough impact to be worth shooting for.

The change in loyalty, on the other hand, would require the line-of-business heads to stop bad-mouthing corporate and each other. You look out the window, noticing the complete absence of flying pigs; check the sports pages and see that the Cubs have not yet won a World Series, and decide the odds of success are best expressed in scientific notation ... with a large and negative exponent.

Never mind.

Take these insights and capture them in the now-complete culture change worksheet (Table 11).

Culture change is, without a doubt, the most difficult aspect of organizational change to master. It's difficult enough when you lead an organization. Achieving it from the side is even harder, because it's a two-stage process: First you have to persuade those who lead the organization of its importance.

Once you've done so, it's no less difficult just because they've agreed to it, because ... culture change is, without a doubt, the most difficult aspect of organizational change to master, for executives no less than for you.

Table 12/ *Business Change Checklist – Culture*

Responsibility	Assignee	Completed
Characterize the culture in the form of situation/response statements, expressing each cultural trait in both positive and negative terms	Project Manager, Business Sponsor, Inner Circle	
Determine which cultural characteristics matter for the change (maximum of 3)	Project Manager, Business Sponsor, Inner Circle	
For the characteristics that matter, describe the desired culture (positive terms only)	Project Manager, Business Sponsor, Inner Circle	
Design changes to the physical and communication/collaboration environments that would encourage the change in culture	Project Manager or delegate	
Determine how leader behavior has led to the current culture, and how it must change to encourage the desired culture	Project Manager	
Assess the importance and impact of the desired culture changes, and how much time would be needed for culture change to start becoming visible	Project Manager	
Decide which changes in leader behavior to pursue	Project Manager, Business Sponsor	
Work with business leaders to make the change happen	Project Manager or Business Sponsor	

CHAPTER 7/

COMMUNICATION PLAN[44]

When citizens of the United States travel abroad, we're notorious for substituting volume for linguistic ability. If someone doesn't speak English at 60 decibels, we must figure, maybe the meaning will get through at 110.

Or maybe not. Which brings up, prematurely, an important communications principle, which is to communicate in your audience's terms, not your own.

It's premature because "communication" consists of four separate responsibilities, and while making sure *you* understand *me* might be at the top of my instinctive list of priorities, it shouldn't be my actual top priority.

Even farther back in line is making sure you agree with me – an outcome far too many people figure will be automatic if only the person they're trying to persuade understands them.

This must be how most people approach persuasion. It's an inescapable conclusion, given how often the most sophisticated approach to persuasion most people show is mind-numbing repetition.

Maybe they learned it watching television commercials.

Enough with the foreshadowing. Let's move forward to the beginning, which is, as usual, defining terms.

Fortunately for us, communication has been defined quite precise-

44 Some of this material was adapted from the chapter on communication in *Leading IT: The Toughest Job in the World* (Bob Lewis, 2004).

ly within the field of information theory. To whit: Communication is the process through which one entity (the sender) transmits information to another entity (the receiver).

Which would be very helpful if we only had a precise definition of information. Luckily, we do: Information is the stuff that reduces uncertainty.

It's a definition that's nearly useful. Not quite, though. Like it or

---

DON'T FORGET TO COMMUNICATE WITH CUSTOMERS AND SUPPLIERS

Some organizational changes will be visible to customers ... the real paying customers who buy the products and services your company sells. Others will be visible to suppliers – the people you rely on (it's always people, no matter how big the company) to keep your company supplied with the raw materials it needs to create its finished products.

To the extent the change you're putting into place will affect them, make sure to include them in your communication plans.

And, don't try to handle this category of communication yourself. For customers, you have a Marketing department. For suppliers you have Purchasing or Supply Chain Management.

That's what they're for. They should be part of the project team already, ready for you to assign responsibility for communicating with customers and suppliers.

Use whoever heads up Marketing as your proxy for the company's customers, and spell out, very explicitly, that you're doing so. Do likewise with Purchasing.

Then keep both departments very well informed of what's going on, and ask that they keep you informed of their communication plans, and coordinate them with you, because ...

... wouldn't it be embarrassing if employees learn something important about what's going to happen from a customer of vendor?

---

not, we all are living in a sea of disinformation, resulting in large numbers of people who are, on any given subject, both certain and wrong.

If a change leader fails to communicate well, many change accepters will be among them, having obtained answers to their questions from unreliable sources, when they could have had an accurate picture of what's going on instead.

Let's refine our definition, then: Information is the stuff that results in an accurate reduction in uncertainty.

In business settings, communication takes four forms[45]:

> *Listening:* Obtaining information from others.
> *Informing:* Providing information to others.
> *Persuading:* Providing information to others in ways designed to change their opinions.
> *Facilitating:* Helping others listen to, inform, and persuade each other.

The rest of this chapter is divided into two sections. Thing of the first as a refresher course in communication techniques, focused on what's most important to support a business change. The second section builds on the first, providing a framework for planning communication tasks.

COMMUNICATION TECHNIQUES

Listening

In general-purpose leadership, listening is a critical skill because performers are the only ones who know What's Really Going On Out There: What customers are saying about the company, for example; how work really gets done; where processes aren't working they way they're supposed to work; and what their colleagues are saying about the company to each other and their friends; to name just a few of the subjects leaders need to be informed about.

Fail to listen and leaders aren't just ignorant. They're willfully ignorant.

When it comes to designing a business change ... when, for example, designing a new-and-improved business process ... it's the performers who know and have to deal with all of the situations the new-and-improved process will have to handle. Any business process designer who doesn't listen to performers is a process design-

---

THE PROXIMITY TRAP

Among the many difficulties you face in organizational listening is the almost unavoidable tendency to listen more to those who have the most access to you.

Whether it's because you like them, or simply because they sit nearby, you converse with some people more than others.

This can lead to minor distortions, or it can cripple your ability to make decisions based on an accurate understanding of What's Really Going On Out There.

In particular, in many organizations access and knowledge are inversely related: People in the field know what's really going on, but they have the hardest time reaching you.

Why do you think decisions that come from headquarters are so dopey so often?

---

45 It does, at times, take additional forms, such as sneering, shouting, belittling and so on. While they are enjoyable pastimes, they won't help you succeed in your change responsibilities, so I'm ignoring them in this chapter.

er for whom you should write a glowing recommendation, to help make sure he or she is quickly and gainfully employed by one of your competitors.

As for you in your role making a business change happen: Change can make people nervous. People who are nervous have questions. People who have questions want answers and will get them from someone.

They won't get their answers from you unless you know what their questions are, and you won't know that unless you listen to them.

Fail to listen and you've taken the first step toward turning change accepters into change resisters.

Or, perhaps, failed to take the first step toward turning change accepters into change supporters.

THE FILTRATION TRAP

Among the human failings most understandable in ourselves and unforgivable in others is the tendency we all have to embrace as strong evidence information that fits our existing biases, while either waving off or nitpicking to death information that conflicts with them.

The cognitive balancing act you have to achieve is a difficult one. If you've thought carefully about a subject and have done your homework, many differing opinions probably aren't worth your time.

It depends how you've done your homework. Those who form an opinion first and research it second are more likely to be gathering ammunition than trying to understand more deeply.

Those who gather evidence first are more likely to make an evidence-driven decision.

To keep yourself on the right side of this challenge, consciously scrutinize any and all evidence and logic that reinforces your opinion more closely than any you disagree with.

Just as important: When you ask questions, pay attention to how you ask them. If your phrasing suggests a preferred answer, rephrase the question, and even if it doesn't, ask the question a few different ways to make sure you aren't biasing what you learn.

Even more important: Find a few people you respect who disagree with you, and listen to them on the subject on a regular basis.

Listening vs organizational listening

In the context of business change management, *listening*, as in making sure you understand what someone is saying to you, isn't the challenge.

The challenge is *organizational listening* – hearing what performers and stakeholders … the organization taken as a whole … are saying and thinking about the change you're responsible for turning into reality.

In the context of business change management you have a few

alternatives for use in organizational listening. You can:
> Have one-on-one or small-group conversations.
> Conduct formal surveys.
> Make use of your personal network.
> Make use of project team members' personal networks.

Conversations

You can, to a limited extent, listen to the organization by having in-dividual conversations. Make King Harry in Shakespeare's *Henry V* your role model. Before the battle of Agincourt he disguised him-self and wandered among his soldiers, mostly listening to what they were talking about. That's how he knew what to say before the bat-tle to inspire them.

I doubt there's any point in disguising yourself. And it's unlikely you'll be facing a situation as dire[46]. The point is to listen to a lot of people. You don't have to be fancy. Choose names at random from the organizational charts of the areas affected by the change, con-tact their managers to ask permission (good manners never go out of style), and schedule one-on-one or small-group meetings.

Then make sure you do more listening than talking. Acknowledge what you hear – express appreciation for every point of view you hear expressed.

And whatever you do, don't use the occasion as an opportunity to argue your own perspective. Don't offer to speak as the Devil's Advocate. At most, after you've heard what everyone else has to say, provide your current thinking about the subject ... that's how you present it ... and make clear your mind is still open to other points of view, including what you've just heard.

Formal surveys

This is another don't-get-too-fancy technique. Your company intra-net probably has the ability to easily set up questionnaires, giving you the results in a form you can bring into Excel.

Keep it brief. Five questions is a good target to shoot for. Some examples:
> How aware are you of the change? (0=What change? 5=I'm on the project team, you idiot!)
> To what extent do you expect to be affected by the change? (0=Not at all; 5=It will completely change my job.)

---

46 It's also unlikely you'll ever achieve anything like King Harry's level of eloquence. Don't worry about it.

> Do you think the change will deliver positive results to the company? (0=Serious harm; 5=Huge improvements all the way around.)
> Do you expect the change to benefit you personally? (0=It will ruin my life; 5=It will make my life a thing of wonder.)
> What could interfere with what we're trying to accomplish, preventing it from succeeding? (Provide room for comments.)
> Do you have any other ideas about the change you'd like to share? (Provide room for comments.)

Send out an e-mail notification to all employees you think will be affected by the change from time to time ... perhaps every month or two. Very important: Emphasize that the system is entirely confidential – you'll never learn who provided which responses.

Personal network

You know a lot of people in the company (and if you don't, you should – it's the single best career management technique you have). The people you know have personal networks of their own.

Ask what they've heard about how employees at different levels and in different areas are reacting to the change. Ask them to keep their ears open and to let you know if they hear anything interesting, making it clear you won't ask them to violate any confidences.

Project team's personal network

Change is accomplished by project teams. Every member of the project team has friends throughout the company too. Ask them to keep their ears to the ground and to let you know what the buzz is about the change.

Informing

When most people hear the word "communicate" they think about informing – presenting information to someone else so they're better-informed than they were before the interchange. As a change leader, when you think about providing information to someone, take a minute to ask yourself if that's really your goal.

Often, people present information because they've unconsciously decided not to provide leadership. "My job is to provide information," according to this way of thinking. "It's up to the listener to draw the right conclusion."

No. If you want someone to draw the right conclusion, you should do your best to persuade them – the subject of the next section. Anything else leaves too much to chance.

When you're leading a business change there are plenty of situations in which informing is precisely the right goal. Remember that

CRITICAL ASSUMPTION

This book isn't about designing business change. It does, however, have to make some assumptions about the change you've designed.

One assumption is that you've done everything you can to create a path to personal success for those employees willing to help make the business change a success.

There might be layoffs. In hard times you might be asking employees to accept reductions in work hours or compensation. You aren't promising nothing but sweetness and light.

But you are providing a path to success, and treating everyone else as compassionately as you can.

This assumption isn't a matter of "doing the right thing," or because this book isn't intended to help bad people.

Providing a clear path to success is a necessary prerequisite to avoiding the most extreme forms and levels of change resistance. If the point isn't clear, go back to the core promise of this book: Employees don't resist change because they're stupid. They resist it because they're smart.

Take, for example, companies that plan to send all IT development work offshore. Included in the project plan are the entirely logical tasks of making sure all applications are fully documented and having the on-shore developers train their offshore replacements in the undocumentable details.

Now ask yourself: If you were one of the on-shore developers, why would you do anything more than the absolute minimum to help with this process?

If you're planning to send work offshore, you'll need a better answer than, "We expect you to behave as professionals." Because your developers, being professionals, will focus as much of their time and effort as they can in finding new opportunities just as fast as they can.

If they're enterprising, they might even all leave at once to form a business that will sell you consulting services, at a premium price, to provide the documentation and training your new offshore partner will so desperately need.

And so ...

This book doesn't include suggestions for any specific answer to the question, "Why should we support this change?" It does rest on the assumption that you have a good answer.

a primary cause of resistance to change is uncertainty. Employees who are uncertain as to whether they'll be able to succeed in their future roles; are uncertain that they even have future roles; or even just aren't all that sure they'll be able to master a new process the way they had mastered the old (often informal) one ... all of these levels of uncertainty could easily cause employees to feel concerned about what your change will do to them.

And yes ... right about now you might reasonably conclude that even here we're in the realm of persuasion: You need to persuade employees they can be successful, will still have a job, and will be able to master the new approach to whatever-it-is. There's no hard line separating informing from persuading. You also might conclude we're in the realm of training, as the best way to persuade someone they can figure something out is to help them do so. There's no hard line separating informing from training, either.

Still, there are plenty of situations that call for more-or-less pure informing, starting with many of the strategies in the stakeholder analysis from chapter 1 and all of the "I" entries in the PACI chart from chapter 2, and including everything you can do to help paint a clear picture of what the future will look like:

> If the management team has figured out what the new organizational chart will look like, everyone affected will want to understand it, where they fit into it, who their new manager is and what he or she will be like to work with.

> When you've figured out where a newly formed or relocated team will sit, everyone on the team will want to know that.

> If, as part of the effort, you're selecting a software package or a consulting partner, every stakeholder will be interested to learn what package they'll be using and consulting partner they'll be working with.

> When you've completed a significant milestone on the project plan, letting everyone know about it will increase their confidence that the change is real and will actually happen.

> Even if there's nothing in particular to report, but a month has passed since the last time you communicated with one or more stakeholder groups, inform them of something, so they know you haven't lost interest or given up.

Which leads to the question of how to communicate effectively. The starting point is the **_umwelt_**.

Communicate within your audience's *umwelt*

What's an *umwelt*? *Umwelt* is a century-old concept introduced to ethology, the study of animal behavior, by Jakob von Uexküll. It's the recognition that every animal exists in a unique perceptual universe that's closed to human beings other than through inference: Much of a bee's world is ultraviolet; a dog's nose does a lot of what we use our eyes to accomplish. Then there are bats, which use sonar, and the electric fish[47] I studied in graduate school, which perceive their world through a sense we lack entirely.

Different people live in different *umwelts* too, although they aren't as hard to imagine as an olfactory universe, let alone an electric one. You've already gone through the trouble of trying to understand your audiences – that's what the stakeholder analysis was for. Go one step further and try to see the world through their eyes and hear it through their ears. Then, you can find a way to present your message so it sounds like an extension of what each audience already knows and believes.

Or at least you can phrase your presentation based on their vocabulary and connect it to their experiences.

If you're communicating with one executive, do everything you can to determine his or her hot buttons: Key motivators, personal and organizational goals, likes and dislikes. If it's a small group, analyze each member this way. If it's a large group, divide it into categories and profile each category.

If in doubt, refer back to the stakeholder analysis. It's your *umwelt* guide.

Decide on the key take-aways

Presenting everything you know is a popular, and thoroughly ineffective approach many experts use when trying to inform the uninformed.

Contrary to popular belief, this usually isn't the result of a presenter who loves to show off. The motivation is far more noble than that. Experts in any subject love their subject – that's why they became an expert in it. And when you love a subject you want your audience to love it, too.

---

47 Didn't I mention this? Electric fish are nifty little critters that produce electrical impulses roughly the same strength as a smoke detector battery and detect them through an array of detectors that cover their skin. They use these impulses to communicate with each other, and to detect objects in their environment. Try to imagine what that experience must be like and you'll gain some appreciation for the significance of the *umwelt* concept.

So the first step in simplifying your message is reminding yourself that your audience doesn't love the subject the way you do. Far from it: They find it complicated, difficult to understand, and probably tedious as well.

The antidote: A focus on clarity rather than completeness.

Simplify your explanation to its essence. The cliché, which regrettably is hard to improve on, is to develop your "elevator speech," which is to say, imagine you and someone important to achieving the goal find yourselves on an elevator. How do you explain what you're trying to achieve before one of you gets off the elevator?

When your goal is to inform, the best formula to help you craft your elevator speech is probably the journalistic who, what, when, where, why, and how. Develop crisp, bulleted answers to each of these questions, not long, rambling ones. Your goal is to inform, not to bore.

Feel free to change the order to fit the circumstances.

Whatever you're trying to explain, you know way too much about it, and you're going to be tempted to explain everything you know.

Resist the temptation. What you have to say is the center of your cosmos, but it's just one asteroid in your audience's solar system.

If you need to impart a lot of information

Sometimes, you have to educate, and not in the context of the training plan. That is, you need to provide a lot of information in a way that helps others become a lot smarter about a subject.

When you do, make use of a technique you might have ignored since your school days: The humble outline.

That's because it's up to you to help your audience navigate the complexities of what you have to say. To do so you have to organize your thinking.

There are those who fail to do so ... who can't be bothered to present their evidence and logic in easy-to-follow ways, instead just dumping it all out there in a stream of consciousness.

People like this act as if it's their audience's responsibility to figure out what they're saying.

But it isn't, and they won't. They won't have the patience for it. They'll just ignore the presenter as someone not worth listening to.

There's a good chance they'll be right.

So organize your presentation. As a general rule, start with a topic sentence that explains what you'll be talking or writing about. Follow it with at least three, and no more than seven subtopics. A nice approach (which you'll find used throughout this book) is to list the subtopics immediately after the topic, then re-state each one separately as a heading, followed by whatever explanation seems appropriate to the situation.

Choose your medium.

Or, better, choose their medium: Your key take-aways and knowledge about your audience's preferred communication styles should determine the medium, not your own preferences. "They should have read their e-mail," is about as useful as any other choice that substitutes how things should be for how they actually are.

If your audience is an executive who wants to look you in the eye, make sure you meet face-to-face. If it's a middle-manager who likes voicemail, use voicemail. If it's a large, diverse group of stakeholders, schedule a group meeting so you can make sure everyone hears the same information presented the same way, and have the opportunity to hear each others' questions and your answers to them.

If they're readers, send them the information in advance of the briefing meeting so they can prepare questions   a tactic that also gives you political cover should anyone complain about being uninformed later on.

And even though you "... like to scribble on the whiteboard while I'm talking," ... that's *your* preference. If your audience will reject your message because whiteboard-scrawling connotes lack of preparation, stuff your preference in the closet and prepare a formal PowerPoint presentation.

Or vice versa, if that fits your audience's preference better.

Use formatting to reinforce your message

When you communicate face-to-face, your vocal intonation and body language deliver as much information as your words. In memos and reports, intonation and body language aren't available to you. That's what formatting is for – to substitute for them. You know what your key take-aways are. How are you going to make sure the reader remembers them?

The act of formatting helps you think things through. Deciding what to bold or italicize, what to put in a bulleted or numbered list, what to separate into a sidebar, what to illustrate through a chart or graphic … or in PowerPoint, whether and how to animate a graphic or bulleted list, and what to put into a "kicker box" at the bottom … these decisions help you think through your message.

Carefully chosen formatting can have another benefit: It constitutes "meta-communication" – communication about the communication. It says you've thought through your communication instead of just blurting everything out. That's a good message to send.

Never forget the law of seven by seven

Information doesn't automatically penetrate the organization just because you delivered it once. The rule of thumb is that if you want something to be known in the organization you must repeat it seven different times, in seven different ways.

In other words, after you explain something one way, wait a day or two and present the same information using different metaphors, illustrations, examples, or evidence.

If that isn't clear, let's try it this way: Different people have different routes to understanding and different speeds of information uptake. By figuring out different ways of explaining things tailored to different learning styles …[48]

Persuading

First, a few points about persuasion in general:
> Everything that matters when you're trying to inform matters even more when you're trying to persuade. Especially, simplicity and clarity are more persuasive than thoroughness and nuance.
> Listen first. Speak second. Introduce the topic and then provide an opportunity for everyone to express their concerns and opinions. Your taking time to listen enhances your credibility. It also makes it easier for everyone else to have the patience to listen to you when it's your turn.
> Do everything you can to make it okay for people to change their minds. "I used to think *x,* then someone persuaded me that *y* is much better" helps everyone else decide changing their minds isn't a sign of weakness. Finding opportunities to say, "Huh – I hadn't thought of that. You've convinced me," helps even more.

---

48 Three repetitions is all I can take. The other four are left as exercises for the reader.

DON'T ARGUE

The art of persuasion has little to do with the discipline of debate.

No, that's too weak. The art of persuasion has nothing at all to do with debating.

Listen to a typical argument and you'll quickly see why debating is useless when trying to persuade. Debating ... arguing, as it's usually practiced ... is about winning and losing, and if, to be persuaded, someone must agree that the other person won, it just isn't going to happen.

Nor should it. Listen to a typical casual argument or formal debate. You'll hear two individuals, each loaded with ammunition, shooting evidentiary and logical bullets at each other like one of those movies where the bad guys empty their Uzis at the hero without a single bullet causing so much as a flesh wound.

What do you think – that someone on the receiving end of all this ammunition, who can't counter it, will reluctantly agree they must have been wrong?

Often, after the shooting is over, they'll track down the evidence, think through the logic, and figure out they were gulled. Debating ammunition includes plenty of half-truths and specious logic that falls apart on close inspection.

An argument is an event. It's about proving you're right. As Randall Munroe, author of the frequently brilliant xkcd once pointed out, that's in contrast to science, whose purpose isn't to show that you're right, it's to become right.

Want to persuade someone? If so, you have to be persuadable, which means creating an atmosphere of shared discovery, not of winning and losing.

> Find opportunities to say it.
>
> And treasure converts. Anyone who used to be on the other side of an issue and has since joined yours is worth more than a PhD thesis when it comes to persuading an audience it's okay to agree with you.

> Know your pronouns:
>   - *I* is a pronoun to be used rarely, and always in a self-deprecating way.
>   - *You* are smart, savvy, and already know this stuff. You're the ones who will make things work.
>   - *We* take on difficult tasks together. We're the ones we can trust and count on.
>   - *They* are the source of all that's wrong with the world. They're stupid, untrustworthy, have no integrity, smell bad, and their mothers dress them funny.

> Use questions more than answers. Doing so helps people

persuade themselves. If you want to play dirty, use push-poll-style questions, like Burger King's famous, "Which would you rather eat – a delicious, flame-broiled piece of chopped steak or a disgusting, greasy, fried, hockey-puck-like disk of ground up cow parts?"

Or as Albert Einstein put it, ninety percent of getting the right answer is asking the right question.

> As an exercise in logic and reason, the plural of anecdote is not data[49]. As an exercise in persuasion, anecdotes ... even manufactured anecdotes ... are far more persuasive than any amount of evidence, and especially they are far more convincing than any statistical evidence.

> And finally, there's benefit. A by-now old joke has it that every employee in your company listens to the same radio station coming to work in the morning: WIIFM, which stands for What's In It For Me?

Want someone to be on your side of an issue? Help them understand how they benefit by doing so.

Earlier in my career I used to try to persuade people using nothing but evidence and logic. Then I read some books on persuasion and learned more effective techniques.

Probably, you're way ahead of me here. You know that to be persuasive you have to deal with emotions, not evidence and logic. As we try to make business change management a more effective discipline, we're going to have to work hard to explain this to some of the people we've all worked with, who figure their responsibility stops when they've explained their point of view, once, and probably in one long unformatted paragraph.

In case you missed what just happened, re-read the last two paragraphs, paying attention to the pronouns. See how well they work?

That's a quick primer on how to persuade in general. In the context of business change you have to persuade stakeholders on only three subjects: The problem, the solution, and the plan.

Selling the problem

Start with the problem. If you can persuade someone that a problem is real you've taken the most difficult step[50]. Everything that follows is a collaborative discussion about how best to solve it.

49 Origin unknown; often attributed to the pharmacologist Frank Kotsonis.
50 Once again, a nod to William Bridges' *Managing Transitions: Making the Most of Change* (1991) – the source of this insight.

Or can be, if you accept the theory of special relativity.

According to Einstein's special theory of relativity, the perspective of all inertial[51] observers is equally valid. Imagine you're parked somewhere in the universe in your spaceship. You see another spaceship approaching you at a constant speed. You figure the other pilot will steer around you.

But he doesn't – he collides with your spaceship, ruining the fenders. You sigh, put on your spacesuit, and float outside to exchange insurance information and ask the other driver in an open-minded and curious way whether he includes any Brussels sprouts among his ancestors.

But before you can ask, you're astonished to hear the other pilot yelling at you, asking what kind of idiot you are for failing to steer around his parked spaceship.

Clearly, the guy is delusional. So you agree to see each other in court.

Which you do. You both testify. The judge listens, shrugs, and explains that both of you are equally right: From your perspective the other spaceship was in motion while you were stationary, but the other pilot's perspective ... that he was stationary while you were in motion ... is just as valid.

Inertial motion is relative, not absolute.

Here's how this plays out in the world of business change management: Just because the business has a problem, it doesn't mean the person you're trying to persuade has a problem.

For example: Many businesses look at their bottom lines from the perspective of return on equity, which, in effect, asks whether the owners would be better off putting their money in an indexed mutual fund or some other comparative benchmark – the so-called "hurdle rate." The CEO of the company you work for does this and sees that while the business is making a profit, it doesn't clear the hurdle rate.

From the CEO's perspective, as steward of the shareholders' investment, this is a problem that must be solved.

An up-and-coming middle manager is assigned the job of business change management, and, understanding the "sell the problem" principle but not Einstein's theory, tries to explain the hurdle rate and the importance of clearing it to the company's employees, as the first step in persuading them an impending business

---

51 An inertial observer is one upon whom no forces are acting.

change is necessary.

To which the employees' respond with one voice, "Let us get this straight: Customers are buying our products, the company is making a profit, our paychecks are clearing and there's no danger they won't clear, and we have a problem? No we don't. We're doing just fine!"

Recall that people don't resist change because they're stupid, but because they're smart – smart enough to understand the difference between a problem for the owners or upper management and their own problems.

You have two choices. The first and better alternative is to find a way to connect the business problem your change is intended to solve to the goals of each stakeholder group. If you can't, don't pretend. Sell the fact of the business problem and explain that while you're doing your best to also make the change as benign as possible for each stakeholder group, management had to make its decision based on what's best for the business.

But connecting the problem to the stakeholder group is, when possible, the superior option, because "It's our problem" is much more powerful than "It's my problem and I'm making it your problem too."

For example:

"Right now, the problem isn't that the business is losing money. It's that we aren't profitable enough. And while that doesn't affect you personally right now, in the long run it will affect you and your colleagues. It works like this: If return on equity is too low, that will push down the price of our stock. If the stock price is too low, it makes us an easy takeover target. And if another company takes us over, all of us will be second-class citizens once the acquisition is done, if we have jobs at all."

See? That wasn't so hard.

Selling the solution

Here's how you sell the solution: Unless you're in a crisis, don't. Instead, once you've sold the problem, solicit ideas for the solution as widely as possible. Parcel out the design decisions. To the extent you can, give every stakeholder or stakeholder group ownership in what you finally decide to implement.

Just as "We have a problem" is more powerful than "I have a problem and I'm making it your problem," so "This is our solution" is more powerful than "Here's my solution, and here's why you should agree with it."

This should sound familiar, because it's a big part of the involvement plan we covered back in chapter 2.

You'll find much of the rest of what you need to do to persuade each stakeholder group in the strategy column of your stakeholder analysis from chapter 1.

There does come a time when the solution is fully baked, and you find yourself having to convince a new stakeholder it's the right solution, or having to convince a fence-sitter that it's time to become part of the solution – here's what it is.

You'll find it easier to do so if you're able to say, with no prevarication or exaggeration, that you involved a lot of people putting the solution together – that it isn't just something that came out of your personal pointy little head.

Selling the plan

The plan is the set of actions the business will take to implement the solution. Mostly, one or a small group of professional project managers should be the ones to put it together. That's what they (you) do for a living, and presumably they (you) are good at it.

There are some decisions you can make more participative. One is whether to use in-house staff, an outside integration team, individual outside consultants, or a combination of the above. This is a strategic decision with broad consequences and no right answer – a perfect candidate not to have your name on as the sole author.

Here's a second one: Governance – how different sorts of decisions will be made, and by whom. Again, so long as there is an answer, what that answer is doesn't matter all that much. Invite the key stakeholders to figure it out, because they're the ones who will have to accept its results when the time comes.

And third: Whether to implement the change steadily in small increments, by flipping a switch, or somewhere in between, for example by breaking the change into a small number of major modules.

Different changes have different logical answers. Again it's a strategic choice that is input to the plan you need to create, as opposed to being the plan you need to create.

Facilitate the discussion; don't try to steer it to a predefined result.

Key messages, with examples for The Change (Centralized purchasing)

The three topics of business change persuasion provide the framework for your key messages: Problem, Solution, Plan. Hone your ability to concisely and persuasively present each one.

General messages

Here are the key messages you'll need all stakeholders to hear:

Problem: Right now, at least one, and often more than one group within each business unit buy office supplies, chairs, smart phones, and all the other bits and pieces of stuff we need every day in the business. These groups use different systems, formats, numbering systems and vendor files, which makes reconciling vendor invoices in Accounts Payable needlessly complicated and expensive. Worse, each group negotiates independently with different vendors, which means we aren't able to take advantage of our size to get the best price and terms.

Short version: We expend too much effort and spend too much for everything we buy.

Solution: We're going to centralize Purchasing, locating it at headquarters and building it on a flexible, but standardized process and system. The new function will report to the Chief Administrative Officer.

As you know, we've already standardized on SAP[52] for our core accounting, including accounts receivable. Using its purchasing module as the foundation for the centralized function is a logical choice. We've evaluated it for suitability, and it looks like it will do the job.

We've involved a lot of people from throughout the business in designing the new process, and we'll be building in a number of features to make using centralized Purchasing as convenient as we can.

[Your name here], who is leading the centralization effort, will become our new Director of Purchasing. He recognizes that centralized functions have a reputation for turning into bureaucratic fiefdoms that are disconnected from business priorities, and plans to conduct regular effectiveness reviews to make sure he is properly supporting the lines of business.

---

52 No endorsement implied, and no product placement fee received. Using a fictional system name ("our XYZ ERP package") seemed fatuous.

Plan: Once we've finished designing the new purchasing process and configuring the software, we'll start the implementation with a one-month pilot at headquarters to give the new process a "shakedown cruise." That will let us find and take care of any rough spots and major glitches. From that point forward we'll roll it out one business unit at a time over a span of a year, at which point the new process will be handling all non-strategic sourcing.

Tailored messages

You aren't finished yet. You've just written the key messages for the overall change. Now it's time to look at each stakeholder group, to see what you might need to add to address any concerns an individual group might have that isn't covered in the blanket message.

Let's use the business unit staff as an example. Here's what we said about them in the stakeholder analysis:

> ➢ *Support/Resistance Factors:*
>   - ► Realistically understand the nature of "synergy targets."
>   - ► Their loyalty is to the business unit – culturally they've never been integrated into the enterprise.
>   - ► Can kill the change through malicious obedience.
> ➢ *Strategy:*
>   - ► Communicate business case thoroughly and repeatedly.
>   - ► Stress the opportunities the project will create (and make sure it creates them, especially for supporters).
>   - ► Be honest about layoff potential; communicate how the company will take care of those laid off early and often (first choice for open positions elsewhere in the company, generous severance packages, and outplacement assistance).

For this group, we should add this to the Solution section:

As the situation stands, each business unit is too small to have treated purchasing as a professional responsibility. Instead, the employees responsible for it have handled it on an ad hoc, *spare-time basis.*

One consequence of centralizing the function is that we'll be able to establish a career path for purchasing professionals.

And, we should add this to the Plan section:

When we first started planning the purchasing centralization effort, we were concerned that it might result in a small number of staff layoffs. We're pleased to report that this will not be necessary.

Right now it appears the new process and department will create positions for three purchasing professionals at headquarters. The staff currently responsible for purchasing within our headquarters and line-of-business staff will be given the opportunity to apply for these positions if they choose to do so. If not, we expect enough growth in each business unit to create plenty of work to keep everyone busy.

Facilitating

Facilitation is a critical skill for any business change manager, and for that matter, for any business leader. That's because of this chain of logic:

1. Nothing works well in business if the people who have to work together don't trust each other.
2. In order for people to trust each other, they have to have confidence in each others' competence and good intentions.
3. In order to have confidence in each other, they have to hear what each other are saying.
4. When frustrated, people are much more likely to talk then to listen.
5. Anyone who thinks someone else won't listen to them won't trust that person.
6. Without your intervention, steps 4 and 5 are inevitable.

While you won't need to develop a facilitation plan, you will need skill at facilitation. It is, as it happens, one of those skills you will never finish developing. It's also a skill for which any account beyond the merest sketch is far too big a subject for this book.

Accordingly, here's a sketch of it – a small grab-bag of techniques to get you started.

> *All meetings have a point:* Agendas are generally a good idea too, although there are some situations where too much structure is counterproductive. If you're going to take an hour of everyone's time, though, be clear about the reason for it.

> *Insist in a positive response:* Not positive as in agree-

ment; positive as in expressing an opinion when a participant asks a question. An impassive expression doesn't indicate agreement, nor, for that matter, does it indicate disagreement. It means the individual in question is trying to avoid public commitment so he or she can ignore whatever agreement the rest of the participants reach.

> *Choose a victim:* When you can't get a group to open up, ask a question of an individual in the room. Then, be quiet … let the silence become uncomfortable. If you have to break the silence, ask the same person the same question again. Your goal is to make it okay to express a thought in that setting.

> *Wait awhile, then shout:* When you can't get a group to stop opening up … when, that is, the number of conversations in the room exceeds the number of people in the room and everyone is enthusiastically expressing themselves to whoever can hear them over the general din … don't try to regain control too quickly. Productive interaction is happening. Within a few minutes, though, shout as loud as you must to get everyone's attention. Don't shout angrily, of course. Be good humored about it; ask everyone to keep it to just one conversation for a bit so everyone gets a sense of what everyone else is thinking.

> *Monitor for non-participants:* Participants with more forceful personalities will naturally dominate most meetings Don't try to prevent this entirely … the cures, like forcing everyone to take turns … are generally worse than the disease.

Do keep an eye out for attendees who are either too shy to push their thoughts into the group or don't care enough to expend the effort, and occasionally call on them, by name, to insist they share a thought or two.

"Insist," by the way, must be done with a smile. You can be coercive, but you shouldn't sound coercive.

> *Use a whiteboard or flip charts:* As participants make points, note them on one or the other. This lets everyone know those points have been made, which is not a small thing. It also gives you automatic note-taking, which will help you for later.

If you're using a whiteboard, when it fills up, shoot it

with your smartphone's camera.

> *Stay out of the middle:* In meetings, ask people to talk to each other, not to you. Outside of meetings, refuse to act as a go-between.

> *Don't participate in content. Do summarize content:* Participating in content is frowned upon among professional facilitators. The theory is that facilitators who participate in content are taking advantage of a privileged position in the meeting.

Don't worry about it. You can express your opinion far more effectively by waiting awhile, then summarizing.

If the participants seem close to consensus you can nail it down by summarizing what you think is the sense of the room: "Here's what I think I've been hearing – does this make sense to everyone?"

If participants are far from consensus, consider summarizing the major positions: "I think I'm hearing three approaches. Am I getting them right?"

And, if the situation appears hopeless and you think you know what the right answer should be, say, "I think I'm hearing three approaches – A, B, and C. It occurs to me we can get the best of all three worlds if we consider doing D instead. What do you think?"

You can get away with this if everyone has had a chance to express their opinion first. Otherwise, you're obviously guilty of sham facilitation, pretending to be trying for consensus when it's clear you walked into the room with the only answer you'll accept.

> *Criticisms are about issues, not each other:* Encourage criticism. Emphasize that everyone's goal is to end up with the best ideas possible, which doesn't happen unless everyone is vocal in their thinking.

About the ideas, that is. "You're an idiot for thinking that," is clearly out of bounds – it's about another participant, not an idea. "That's a stupid idea," is also out of bounds. While a jailhouse lawyer might claim it's a statement about an idea; that's being disingenuous. It's personal.

"I disagree; here's why," isn't just in bounds, it's to be encouraged.

Also emphasize that this is a collaboration, not an argument: Trying to win is against the rules. Trying to make good ideas better is the point, and when you do so everyone wins.

> *Allow some repetition, but not too much of it:* It's okay for someone to make a point more than once. It might even be a good idea, if an early but important thought is getting lost in the shuffle as a conversation goes on.

Too much repetition, though, quickly becomes tedious. Use the whiteboard: Point to the idea where you've already written it down, and ask, "Is what you're saying different from this point right here? Because if it isn't, we've already captured it."

> *When the time comes, perform a consensus check:* Make it official. Announce to everyone that it appears the room has reached a conclusion. State it. Write it down. Then go around the room, asking everyone, in turn, if they … not if they agree with it, but if they agree to it, which isn't the same thing.

> *Have a parking lot:* Sometimes, a participant gets stuck. He or she has had an idea … it might be a good idea, it might be completely boneheaded, and either way it's about a topic that has nothing at all to do with what you're trying to accomplish.

Write it down in a "parking lot" area for future reference, and promise to return to it in a future meeting.

Then, make sure you actually do return to it. Your credibility is at stake.

COMMUNICATION PLAN

Under stress, human beings communicate less rather than more. We shut down information inputs … listening … so we can concentrate. We stop sharing information … informing … because that takes too much time and we don't think we have any.

And, we stop trying to persuade, instead using our authority, even though the use of authority gets us nothing better than obedience, when what we need is at least buy-in; and enthusiasm would be better.

When you're trying to change an organization, you will be under constant stress. That's the nature of the beast. So the very human tendency to communicate less will always be with you.

Fight it.

The best way to fight it is to include communication tasks in the project plan, so you and everyone else knows who is supposed to handle them and when they're supposed to happen.

It's important, because without communication, the other six components of business change management will be just so many trees falling in uninhabited forests.

Here are the components of your plan:

Organizational listening plan

For high-level executives, organizational listening is a big, hairy, complicated deal. They need a far wider range of information; need it on a regular basis; and can't trust any single channel to provide an accurate, unbiased, nuanced and timely view.

Your needs are more easily met. What's most important is to remember, when you're under time, financial, and political pressure, to invest the effort to do it.

Make the time. Remember the stakeholder analysis from back in chapter 1? You need to know what the various stakeholder groups are thinking about what you're trying to accomplish, because if you don't, you could accidentally deliver exactly the wrong message to exactly the wrong group, and your whole change program will blow up in your face.

Here's how to make the time: Build organizational listening into the project.

For informal listening ... listening through everyone's personal networks ... include a "What's the buzz?" review into the project team's weekly status meetings, and assign every team member responsibility for keeping track of the buzz within their circle of friends and acquaintances.

Beyond that, add frequent touch-base meetings with key stakeholders to your personal calendar, to let them know you're still interested in what they have to say.

The more formal listening activities, such as surveys and roundtable discussions, will probably be milestone-driven rather than occurring on a periodic schedule. Decide which milestones should drive them, and build them into the project plan.

Information and persuasion plan

From a planning perspective, informing and persuading have

identical characteristics, and share one characteristic with listening: Your choices are to either build tasks into the project plan or fail to do them well.

Build events whose goal is to inform and persuade into the project schedule. Determine which project milestones will trigger the need.

Add periodic communication on top of that ... regular project updates. These accomplish two goals: They provide important information to people who will be wondering what's going on, and they remind everyone that you're the authoritative source of information on this subject, ready to answer any questions anyone might have.

Review key messages with the project team as well. Every time they touch base with their circle of friends and acquaintances as part of their organizational listening responsibilities, they'll be answering questions at the same time.

It's a good idea to make sure all team members respond to the same questions the same way. This doesn't mean they have to have scripted responses that are word-for-word identical. That will just make everyone sound like a phony.

It's the content that should be coordinated, which in turn should be a natural byproduct of your responsibility, as a project manager, to make sure all team members understand the project the same way.

Orchestration

In many situations, sequence matters: If you don't take great care to orchestrate who receives information in what order, you'll cause offense, consternation, and in extreme circumstances, chaos.

Consider a reorganization (as opposed to a realignment; see chapter 5 if you need to refresh your memory as to the differences). There are lots of ways to sequence the announcement wrong and only one or two ways to sequence it well.

Start with the wisdom of Benjamin Franklin, who once said, "Three can keep a secret if two are dead." Once you announce the reorganization to anyone, you've announced it to everyone in a very short period of time no matter how strongly you emphasize the need for discretion.

Now imagine you mention to one of the future managers that she'll be in charge of a particular department (and as it's a reorganization this department doesn't yet currently exist). She'll start thinking about who she'll want working for her, and might, discreetly, ask one or two of her favorites if, hypothetically, they'd be interested.

As is the case with neutrons liberated by the fission of a uranium atom, which go on to cause the fission of additional nuclei, this information will spread, becoming distorted as it does, until everyone "knows" something about the upcoming reorganization.

That's what not to do. Here's what to do instead – an example of a carefully orchestrated sequence of informational events, very similar to one we used with a client to announce the reorganization of a Sales department. It's here to illustrate how to think through the staging of complex informational situations, not as *the* way to announce a reorganization::

1. ***Inform the CEO face-to-face.*** You might have already done so, if the CEO is listed as an Approver in the involvement plan. If not, give a full walk-through. Sell the problem again – briefly, as a reminder, to set the stage. Present the logic behind the organizational plan, who you've selected for the management roles, and the process you either have or plan to go through to transition staff into their new roles.

   You and the business sponsor should handle this briefing together. Decide who will present what in advance – this presentation should give every appearance of being thoughtful and well-prepared.

2. ***Inform the executive team via e-mail and voice mail.*** Use voice mail to let them know that the reorganization will be made public and when, and to alert them that they'll find the details in their e-mail inbox.

3. ***Inform the new management team, as a group, of their new responsibilities.*** Give them the same information you delivered to the CEO, and facilitate a short conversation regarding how they need to transition responsibilities to each other as a result of their change in roles.

   Finally, ask them to please … please! … say nothing to anyone about this until the all-hands announcement that will take place later in the day. It's a matter of courtesy, because between now and then you and the business sponsor will be informing those who had expressed interest in management roles, including anyone who had been a manager in the old organization and won't be a manager in the new one, that they were not selected.

4. ***Inform everyone who will be disappointed.*** These should be short (10 to 15 minute) one-on-one conversations. You and the business sponsor (you'll divide these between you) should be compassionate without being disingenuous: If someone didn't make the cut because you decided they would not have been successful in the new role, be clear about this without being brutal about it.

Let each individual know what their new role will be, who they will be reporting to, and that you have confidence that they'll succeed in it, and that it's valuable.

Explain the impact on their future compensation, too – that will be a matter of significant concern. Sometimes that means explaining that the company will be freezing their compensation at its current level, because it is at or beyond the top of the salary range for their new responsibilities. If so, be as positive in your phrasing as possible ("The company isn't asking you to accept a reduction in your compensation. Here's what it does mean, though.")

5. ***Announce the new organization to all employees in the new organization in an all-hands meeting.***

This will be the same presentation you gave the CEO, minus any overly candid assessments of those who lost ground. If you've already slotted staff into the new organization, announce who will be reporting where, and to whom; also let them know that immediately after the all-hands they'll be meeting with their new managers.

If you haven't decided who will report where, let everyone know what the process of deciding this will be like.

Make sure to introduce the new management team. Unless the reorganization is being accompanied by layoffs, make even surer that the whole announcement has an upbeat tone to it. This is good news you're announcing.

If there will be layoffs, acknowledge the fact in the meeting, let everyone know what the company will be doing for the departing employees, and take this opportunity to *sell the problem*. Especially if there's bad news attached to the announcement, you're no longer simply providing information. You're engaged in persuasion.

6. ***The new managers conduct department meetings.***
   As mentioned in point 5, if you announced everyone's new assignments in the all-hands, follow it immediately with individual department meetings, to get the new organization launched on the right foot. The new managers should include an overview of any associated process changes, in particular in the context of how they will affect those in their departments.

7. ***Inform the rest of the company.*** Distribute the same e-mail you provided to the executive team to everyone else in the company. Some will be very interested. Others will have no interest at all; even these employees might take offense at being ignored. It costs you nothing to let them know what's going on.

8. ***Inform affected customers and suppliers.*** This responsibility belongs to Marketing and Purchasing (or Supply Chain Management), respectively. Orchestrating the outside announcement with your internal announcements is your responsibility.

Not everyone considers this sort of carefully structured sequence of events to be a natural, or even desirable. They prefer a more *ad hoc*, casual, organic approach. The response is the same as it is to any decisions on the part of a business leader that's based on personal preference or style, which is:

Their style and personal preference doesn't matter. Their responsibility is to their organization, not the other way around, which means they have an obligation to do what will work best, not what they like best.

That being the case, if the situation calls for a carefully orchestrated announcement sequence, that's what they must do.

Facilitation plan

For the most part, facilitation is something you do as part of any business meeting in which you participate, rather than something you plan separately.

For the most part. As facilitation is the process of making sure people communicate with each other, it's worth your time to think through who needs to communicate well with whom, and schedule situations in which they're required to do so, with you present to help keep things smooth.

This is especially true in politically challenging circumstances, and when individuals with bad chemistry or bad history will have to find a way to work together if your change is to be successful.

What's required might be nothing more than an occasional reminder that person A needs to let person B know about something.

Or, as might be the case with two teams that distrust each other because the organization operates in uncooperative silos, you'll need to schedule regular meetings in which members of the distrustful factions are forced to collaborate, and in doing so learn that they can successfully collaborate.

CREATING A FORMAL COMMUNICATION PLAN

Here's how to go about constructing the formal plan. It's a sequence of topics, each of which logically leads to the next:

> *Triggering event:* Whatever is driving the need to communicate, whether it's a project milestone or one month from the last parallel communiqué – triggering events may be nothing more than the passage of time.

> *Audience:* The individual or stakeholder group that is the target of a communication within a triggering event. Triggering events can, and often do lead to the need to communicate with multiple audiences.

> Refer back to your involvement plan to make sure you don't neglect any stakeholder groups that deserve attention.

> *Key issues:* The WIIFM factor ("What's In It For Me," in case you missed it the first time): Whatever you think each audience will care enough the most with respect to the triggering event. Each audience can have between one and no more than five key issues. Any more than five and they aren't key anymore.

> You've done a lot of the preparatory work for this section in the stakeholder analysis, described there as "Support/ Resistance Factors." Make use of it.

> *Desired outcomes:* Form follows function, which means you can't effectively plan a communication if you don't know what result you want.

> *Document/Meeting/Agenda topic:* If it's an e-mail, the Subject. If it's a report, the Title. If it's for a meeting, what you'd call it on the appointment calendar. If it's one topic among many for a meeting, how you'll identify it on the meeting agenda.

> *Vehicle:* The communications medium you'll use for each audience.

> *Messages:* The key messages or take-homes you'll deliver to each audience in order to achieve the desired outcomes.

> *Assignee:* Who's responsible. Sometimes, it's more than one person, for example if one person will prepare an e-mail to be sent under an executive's name.

> *Date planned:* When you want the communication to happen.

> *Actual date:* When it really happens.

The communication planning form is nothing more than a tool. To ensure everything on the form actually takes place, it's a good idea to include each row as a task on the project schedule, to be tracked along with every other project task that must be performed in order for the project to be considered complete.

The Change (Centralized Purchasing)

To illustrate how to go about the planning process, we'll take one last look at centralized purchasing, focusing on a specific milestone, namely, the *Triggering Event* of launching the pilot project at corporate headquarters, providing two examples – the CEO and business unit heads.

Audience: CEO

> *Key issues (from stakeholder analysis):*
> ▶ His neck is on the line with the board of directors.
> ▶ Bigger profits mean bigger bonuses.
> ▶ He likes being liked, so linking him too strongly to the layoffs could turn him into a resister.
> ▶ But, an implementation that fails to deliver measurable financial benefits will definitely turn him into a resister.

> *Desired outcomes:*
> ▶ Confidence the effort will be successful.
> ▶ Confidence that this effort will create momentum

and credibility for centralizing additional processes.

▶ Confidence that even though the initially expected layoffs won't take place, there still will be measureable financial benefits coming out of the process.

▶ Communication of support from the CEO to the business unit heads, and a reminder to them that success will result in a positive impact on their annual bonus.

> *Meeting topic:* Centralized purchasing pre-pilot executive briefing.

> *Vehicle:* Face-to-face meeting with CEO, business sponsor and project manager.

> *Messages:*

▶ We're on track for a successful pilot.

▶ While the financial opportunity isn't huge, analysis shows significant opportunities for savings in two areas – better discounts from vendors, and reduced workload in accounts payable which could lead to staffing reductions or redeployments later on.

▶ The CEO's leadership is important right now, to make sure the business unit heads are publicly supportive.

> *Assignee:* You (project manager) to prepare; you and the business sponsor (CAO) to present and discuss.

> *Date scheduled:* First in sequence of communication events.

Audience: Business Unit Heads

> *Key Issues (from stakeholder analysis):*

▶ See this project as a reduction in their authority and loss of autonomy.

▶ All three suffer from serious cases of the "Not Invented Here" syndrome.

▶ All three are money-motivated.

> *Desired outcomes:*

▶ Persuade them to reassure their organizations that this change will be workable for them, and really, not a big deal.

> ► Get their buy-in that they have to visibly use the new process instead of bypassing it.
> ► Focus them on the positive impact on their annual bonuses.

> *Meeting topic:* Centralized purchasing pre-pilot executive briefing.

> *Vehicles:*
> ► Web conference for the formal briefing.
> ► Private call from the CEO to deliver the bonus message.

> *Messages:*
> ► We're on track for a successful pilot.
> ► Thanks for providing key staff members to help with the design effort.
> ► While the financial opportunity isn't huge, analysis shows significant opportunities for savings through better discounts from vendors.
> ► Their leadership is essential – especially, their public willingness to use the new process.

> *Assignee:*
> ► Formal web conference: You (project manager) to prepare; you and the business sponsor (CAO) to present and discuss.
> ► Informal call: CEO

> *Date scheduled:* Immediately following CEO briefing.

Communication planning form

To help you keep this under control, here's (drum roll please) ... a form (Table 13). As with the other forms in this book, the point isn't filling out the form, and if you find some other approach to keeping your thoughts organized to be more helpful, that's fine. It's keeping things straight that matters.

Table 13/ Communication planning form

Triggering event	Audience	Key issues	Desired outcomes	Document/ meeting/ agenda topic	Vehicle	Messages	Assignee	Date Planned	Actual
Pilot launch	CEO	> His neck is on the line w/BoD. > Bonus impact. > Likes being liked. > Measurable financial benefits are essential.	> Confidence in success. > Confidence in momentum for further centralization. > Confidence in measureable financial benefits. > Agreement to communicate need for support to business unit heads.	Centralized purchasing pre-pilot executive briefing.	Face-to-face briefing	> Pilot is on track. > Savings in two areas – better discounts and reduced A/P workload. > Need him to make sure the business unit heads are publicly supportive.	> Project Manager > Business Sponsor	First in sequence.	
	Business Unit Heads	> Loss of authority and autonomy. > "Not Invented Here" syndrome. > All three are money-motivated.	> Reassure their organizations it will work and isn't a big deal. > Agree to visibly use the new process. > Remind them of bonus impact.	Centralized purchasing pre-pilot executive briefing.	Web conference + CEO calls	> Pilot is on track. > Their staff member participants helped and approve of the design. > Savings from better discounts. > They need to visibly use the new process.	> Web conference: > Project Manager > Business Sponsor > Private calls > CEO	Immediately after the CEO briefing.	
	Others	Left as exercise for the reader.							
Conclusion of pilot.									
Business Unit Rollout #1									
...									

Table 14/ *Business change checklist – Communications*

Responsibility	Assignee	Completed
Develop and communicate informal organizational listening assignments	Project Manager	
Develop and administer formal employee surveys	HR Project Team representative	
Schedule employee listening roundtables	Project Manager	
Establish timetable and responsibility for periodic project updates for general employees and specific stakeholders and stakeholder groups	Project Manager, Communication Specialist	
Identify project milestones that should trigger communication events	Project Manager, Communication Specialist	
Develop communication content	Communication Specialist, reviewed by Project Manager and Business Sponsor	
Create orchestration plans for complex announcements	Project Manager, Business Sponsor	
Create consolidated communication plan and build tasks into project schedule	Project Manager	

CHAPTER 8/

CONSOLIDATED BUSINESS CHANGE CHECKLIST

EPILOG

There you have it. Seven steps to heaven, or at least seven tools for your business change toolbox, along with an instruction manual for their use.

Seem overwhelming? It is overwhelming, especially if you find yourself playing catch-up, as one client did a few years back, waking up to the need for business change management just as the software was entering the testing phase.

By then it's too late to manage business change. All you can do is market it to the best of your ability.

Don't do that.

HOW TO NOT BE OVERWHELMED

Now that you see the whole picture, here's how to avoid being overcome with dread and angst: Build your business change management plan a piece at a time, as part of the process of designing and planning the change itself.

That is, for every element of the change, ask:

> Which stakeholders will this affect, how, and how are they likely to react when they learn of it?
> Who should we involve in this, and how?
> For this change element, how will we know if we've been successful?
> What aspects of the organization are put together in a way

that they're in conflict with this change element, and what can we do to align them better?

> How will we make sure employees are competent to take care of this element of the change?

> Is what we're designing consistent with our business culture? If not, what are we going to do about it?

> Who needs to know about this, when do they need to know, and what's the best way to persuade them it's the optimal course of action?

> How are we going to know What's Going On Out There so we can defuse potential opposition before it builds up a big enough head of steam to clobber us?

INTEGRATING BUSINESS CHANGE MANAGEMENT INTO PROJECT MANAGEMENT

What a classy-sounding topic! What a straightforward responsibility to address.

Really, there's nothing to it. As you come up with answers to these questions, turn them into specific tasks, decide who will be responsible for performing them, and add them to the project schedule.

If you do, they'll get done. If you don't, you'll wake up one day, shortly before deployment, wishing you'd done more to gain acceptance for the change throughout the organization.

EVALUATION

Managing business change is a skill for which there is no such thing as good enough. At one end of the scale is implementing a minor change in procedure and organization, like centralizing purchasing in a mid-size corporation.

At the other end of the scale is the caliber of diplomacy and Machiavellianism required to achieve peace in the Middle East.

This is true both in the sense of individual competence (that would be you) and organizational competence: While this book has presented the discipline as something for which an individual takes responsibility, it's best if the whole organization works to achieve increasingly high levels of competence at smoothly implemented change.

That being the case, at the end of each discrete change effort it's worth taking the time to conduct a debriefing session, in which the ringleaders reconvene to ask themselves three questions:

1. ***What worked well?*** Whatever worked well is worth
    adding to the organization's body of knowledge,
    whether it's formally maintained as an institutional
    knowledge base or informally spread through folklore.

2. ***What didn't work well?*** Anything that flopped is worth
    analyzing to determine what went wrong. If a concept
    simply failed, ban it from the next change effort. If the
    concept appears valid for some circumstances but not
    others, "others" including the just-completed change
    effort, add that understanding to the body of knowledge.

    And if the problem was bad execution, take some time
    to figure out what would have been different about good
    execution.

3. ***What new ideas occurred to participants during the***
    change? This book is just a starting point — the bare
    bones of the discipline. As a natural part of getting
    things done, it's likely new ways of reducing resistance
    and building support will occur to you and your
    colleagues.

    Find out what they are, and make sure to build them
    into the plan for the next change.

Business change management is a practice, not a process. There's
no recipe or magic potion that guarantees success, just a formula for
improving the odds.

That formula is, as is always the case with a practice, the knowledge, experience, skill, and judgment of the practitioner.

That's why it's called a practice, in fact: The only way to become good at it is to practice.

THE CHANGE (CENTRALIZED PURCHASING)

As we've been following consolidation of purchasing to a centralized function as a way to illustrate the principles of business change
management, I thought you'd like to know how it came out.

The pilot project went off without a hitch. Corporate headquarters adapted to the new process as if it had been heavily sprayed
with WD-40, and at the end of the 30-day trial period, the project
manager was treated to a one-month all-expenses paid Caribbean
cruise, funded by contributions made by grateful employees
throughout the company.

Then the project manager woke up, showered, dressed, had breakfast, and went to the office, happy that so far the first business unit roll-out felt more like a minor sinus headache than a migraine.

AND FINALLY ...

What's most frustrating about managing business change well is that it has more in common with quality than with excellence: Fail to do it and everyone will notice its absence, and fault you for the ragged or entirely botched implementation of their brilliant plan.

Manage business change well, on the other hand, and most likely nobody will notice.

Unless, that is, they have experience with other business change efforts that weren't as professionally handled.

Why put yourself through this? Wouldn't it be easier to just push in the change and let whoever is going to complain go ahead and complain?

Well, no. First of all, the alternative to managing business change well is to participate in the blamestorming that will inevitably accompany every rough spot in the implementation. While fun, blamestorming does eventually lose its appeal.

The better reason to perfect your business change management skills is this: After you've led a few successful business changes, the executives in your company are likely to notice ... not that you've "managed business change well," but that you seem to be an effective leader.

Acquiring a reputation for effective leadership? That's worth some investment.

Table 15/ Consolidated business change checklist

Component	Responsibility	Assignee	Completed
Stakeholder analysis	List affected stakeholders and stakeholder groups	Project Manager, Business Sponsor, Champion(s)	
	List factors likely to cause support or resistance for each stakeholder and stakeholder group	Project Manager, Business Sponsor, Champion(s)	
	Assess each stakeholder/ stakeholder group's impact	Project Manager, Business Sponsor	
	Develop strategies for each stakeholder and stakeholder group	Project Manager, Business Sponsor	
Involvement plan	Review stakeholder analysis for specific involvement requirements	Project Manager, Business Sponsor	
	List major change design decisions and work threads	Project Manager	
	Allocate design decisions and work threads (Perform and Approve) to stakeholder groups based on stakeholder analysis and the intrinsic logic of each assignment	Project Manager (Perform); Business Sponsor (Consult and Approve)	
	Fill in involvement plan gaps with Consult and Inform indications based on the possibility of interest and expertise	Project Manager	
	Incorporate involvement plan assignments and approvals into project plan(s)	Project Manager	
Metrics plan	Determine expected bottom-line benefits: Revenue, cost, and/or risk.	Business Sponsor	
	Define business outcomes expected to yield the bottom-line benefits.	Business Sponsor	
	Rank internal effectiveness parameters (fixed cost, unit cost, cycle time, throughput, quality, excellence) in order of impact on business outcomes.	Business Sponsor, Change Design Team	
	Design metrics to gauge improvement in the key internal effectiveness parameters.	Business Sponsor, Project Manager or delegate	
	Design metrics to gauge delivery of business outcomes (and, optionally, to demonstrate the connection between internal effectiveness improvements and the business outcomes).	Business Sponsor, Project Manager or delegate	
	Optional: Develop analytics to demonstrate connection between business outcomes and bottom-line benefits.	Business Sponsor, Project Manager or delegate	
	Optional: Establish targets for one or more metrics.	Business Sponsor	
	Design system enhancements to support metrics reporting and add to the system specifications.	Project Manager or delegate	
	Perform final metrics plan review for proper balance between parsimony and completeness.	Business Sponsor and Project Manager	

Table 15/ *Consolidated business change checklist* - *Continued*

Component	Responsibility	Assignee	Completed
Structure plan	Determine[53] organizational strategy	CEO, Executive Team, Project Manager, Business Sponsor	
	For shared services groups, determine service responsibilities and areas of authority	CEO, Shared Services Group Heads, Project Manager, Business Sponsor	
	Determine the "unit of optimization" – generally either the enterprise or business unit levels	CEO, Project Manager, Business Sponsor	
	Design/recommend organizational solution for affected areas of the business; identify solution as realignment, reorganization, or integration	Project Manager, Business Sponsor (Recommend), CEO (Approve)	
	Select managers	Head of affected organizational area(s)	
	Develop transition plan	Project Manager, Business Sponsor, affected executives and managers	
	Design new facilities	Affected Operational Managers, Facilities Manager	
	Document current official and unofficial governance processes associated with the business change	Project Manager, Project Team	
	Design new governance processes, incorporating them into the new process design(s)	Project Manager, Project Team	
	Determine necessary accounting and budgeting changes	Financial Analyst	
	Modify executive, management, and staff compensation and performance evaluation criteria for consistency with the changed way of operating	Project Manager, Operational Managers, Human Resources	
Training plan	Training professional(s) assigned to project	Project Manager	
	Training focus: How to perform new roles, using the new tools	Trainers	
	Training includes context, not just skills	Trainers	
	Floorwalkers assigned	Project Manager	
	Transition training developed	Project Manager	
	Coping skills training developed	Human Resources	
	Stakeholder training program developed	Depends on Stakeholder	
	Training scheduled (1 – 2 weeks prior to deployment)	Project Manager	

---

53   "Determine might be a matter of discovery, if the business change won't change this and will have to conform to it. Or, it might be a matter of design, if the business change is large enough in scope to call the current state into question.

Table 15/ Consolidated business change checklist - Continued

Component	Responsibility	Assignee	Completed
Culture plan	Characterize the culture in the form of situation/response statements, expressing each cultural trait in both positive and negative terms	Project Manager, Business Sponsor, Inner Circle	
	Determine which cultural characteristics matter for the change (maximum of 3)	Project Manager, Business Sponsor, Inner Circle	
	For the characteristics that matter, describe the desired culture (positive terms only)	Project Manager, Business Sponsor, Inner Circle	
	Design changes to the physical and communication/collaboration environments that would encourage the change in culture	Project Manager or delegate	
	Determine how leader behavior has led to the current culture, and how it must change to encourage the desired culture	Project Manager	
	Assess the importance and impact of the desired culture changes, and how much time would be needed for culture change to start becoming visible	Project Manager	
	Decide which changes in leader behavior to pursue	Project Manager, Business Sponsor	
	Work with business leaders to make the change happen	Project Manager or Business Sponsor	
Communication plan	Develop and communicate informal organizational listening assignments	Project Manager	
	Develop and administer formal employee surveys	HR Project Team representative	
	Schedule employee listening roundtables	Project Manager	
	Establish timetable and responsibility for periodic project updates for general employees and specific stakeholders and stakeholder groups	Project Manager, Communication Specialist	
	Identify project milestones that should trigger communication events	Project Manager, Communication Specialist	
	Develop communication content	Communication Specialist, reviewed by Project Manager and Business Sponsor	
	Create orchestration plans for complex announcements	Project Manager, Business Sponsor	
	Create consolidated communication plan and build tasks into project schedule	Project Manager